# MACMILLAN MASTER GUIDES

# MEASURE FOR MEASURE

# BY WILLIAM SHAKESPEARE

## MARK LILLY

*with an Introduction by*
HAROLD BROOKS

**M**
MACMILLAN
EDUCATION

First edition 1986

Published by
MACMILLAN EDUCATION LTD
Houndmills, Basingstoke, Hampshire RG21 2XS
and London
Companies and representatives
throughout the world


Typeset in Great Britain by
TECSET, Sutton, Surrey


Printed in Hong Kong

ISBN 0-333-41710-0 (Pbk)
ISBN 0-333-41711-9 (Export)

# CONTENTS

# GENERAL EDITOR'S PREFACE

The aim of the Macmillan Master Guides is to help you to appreciate the book you are studying by providing information about it and by suggesting ways of reading and thinking about it which will lead to a fuller under-standing. The section on the writer's life and background has been designed to illustrate those aspects of the writer's life which have influenced the work, and to place it in its personal and literary context. The summaries and critical commentary are of special importance in that each brief summary of the action is followed by an examination of the significant critical points. The space which might have been given to repetitive explana-tory notes has been devoted to a detailed analysis of the kind of passage which might confront you in an examination. Literary criticism is con-cerned with both the broader aspects of the work being studied and with its detail. The ideas which meet us in reading a great work of literature, and their relevance to us today, are an essential part of our study, and our Guides look at the thought of their subject in some detail. But just as essential is the craft with which the writer has constructed his work of art, and this may be considered under several technical headings – charac-terisation, language, style and stagecraft, for example.

The authors of these Guides are all teachers and writers of wide ex-perience, and they have chosen to write about books they admire and know well in the belief that they can communicate their admiration to you. But you yourself must read and know intimately the book you are studying. No one can do that for you. You should see this book as a lamp-post. Use it to shed light, not to lean against. If you know your text and know what it is saying about life, and how it says it, then you will enjoy it, and there is no better way of passing an examination in literature.

JAMES GIBSON

# AN INTRODUCTION TO THE
# STUDY OF
# SHAKESPEARE'S PLAYS

A play as a work of art exists to the full only when performed. It must hold the audience's attention throughout the performance, and, unlike a novel, it can't be put down and taken up again. It is important to experience the play as if you are seeing it on the stage for the first time, and you should begin by reading it straight through. Shakespeare builds a play in dramatic units which may be divided into smaller subdivisions, or episodes, marked off by exits and entrances and lasting as long as the same actors are on the stage. Study it unit by unit.

The first unit provides the exposition which is designed to put the audience into the picture. In the second unit we see the forward movement of the play as one situation changes into another. The last unit in a tragedy or a tragical play will bring the catastrophe and in comedy – and some of the history plays – an unravelling of the complications, what is called a *dénouement*.

The onward movement of the play from start to finish is its progressive structure. We see the chain of cause and effect (the plot) and the progressive revelation and development of character. The people, their characters and their motives drive the plot forward in a series of scenes which are carefully planned to give variety of pace and excitement. We notice fast-moving and slower-moving episodes, tension mounting and slackening, and alternate fear and hope for the characters we favour. Full-stage scenes, such as stately councils and processions or turbulent mobs, contrast with scenes of small groups of even single speakers. Each of the scenes presents a deed or event which changes the situation. In performance, entrances and exits and stage actions are physical facts, with more impact than on the page. That impact Shakespeare relied upon, and we must restore it by an effort of the imagination.

Shakespeare's language is just as diverse. Quickfire dialogue is followed by long speeches, and verse changes to prose. There is a wide range of speech – formal, colloquial, dialect, 'Mummerset' and the broken English of foreigners, for example. Songs, instrumental music, and the noise of battle, revelry and tempest, all extend the range of dramatic expression. The dramatic use of language is enhanced by skilful stagecraft, by costumes, by properties such as beds, swords and Yorick's skull, by such stage business as kneeling, embracing and giving money, and by use of such features of the stage structure as the balcony and the trapdoor.

By these means Shakespeare's people are brought vividly to life and cleverly individualised. But though they have much to tell us about human nature, we must never forget that they are characters in a play, not in real life. And remember, they exist to enact the play, not the play to portray *them.*

Shakespeare groups his characters so that they form a pattern, and it is useful to draw a diagram showing this. Sometimes a linking character has dealings with each group. The pattern of persons belong to the symmetric structure of the play, and its dramatic unity is reinforced and enriched by a pattern of resemblances and contrasts; for instance, between characters, scenes, recurrent kinds of imagery, and words. It is not enough just to notice a feature that belongs to the symmetric structure, you should ask what its relevance is to the play as a whole and to the play's ideas.

These ideas and the dramatising of them in a central theme, or several related to each other, are a principal source of the dramatic unity. In order to see what themes are present and important, look, as before, for pattern. Observe the place in it of the leading character. In tragedy this will be the protagonist, in comedy heroes and heroines, together with those in conflict or contrast with them. In *Henry IV Part I*, Prince Hal is being educated for kingship and has a correct estimate of honour, while Falstaff despises honour, and Hotspur makes an idol of it. Pick out the episodes of great intensity as, for example, in *King Lear* where the theme of spiritual blindness is objectified in the blinding of Gloucester, and similarly, note the emphases given by dramatic poetry as in Prospero's 'Our revels now are ended. . .' or unforgettable utterances such as Lear's 'Is there any cause in Nature that makes these hard hearts?' Striking stage-pictures such as that of Hamlet behind the King at prayer will point to leading themes, as will all the parallels and recurrences, including those of phrase and imagery. See whether, in the play you are studying, themes known to be favourites with Shakespeare are prominent, themes such as those of order and disorder, relationships disrupted by mistakes about identity, and appearance and reality. The latter were bound to fascinate Shakespeare whose theatrical art worked by means of illusions which pointed beyond the surface of actual life to underlying truths. In looking at themes beware of attempts to make the play fit some orthodoxy a critic believes in – Freudian perhaps, or Marxist, or dogmatic Christian theology – and remember that its ideas, though they often have a bearing on ours, are Elizabethan.

Some of Shakespeare's greatness lies in the good parts he wrote for the actors. In his demands upon them, and the opportunities he provided, he bore their professional skills in mind and made use of their physical prowess, relished by a public accustomed to judge fencing and wrestling as expertly as we today judge football and tennis. As a member of the professional group of players called the Chamberlain's Men he knew each actor he was writing for. To play his women he had highly-trained boys. As paired heroines they were often contrasted, short with tall, for example, or one vivacious and enterprising, the other more conventionally feminine.

Richard Burbage, the company's leading man, was famous as a great tragic actor, and he took leading roles in seven of Shakespeare's *tragedies*. Though each of the seven has its own distinctiveness, we shall find at the centre of all of them a tragic protagonist possessing tragic greatness, not just one 'tragic flaw' but a tragic vulnerability. He will have a character which makes him unfit to cope with the tragic stiuations confronting him, so that his tragic errors bring down upon him tragic suffering and finally a tragic catastrophe. Normally, both the suffering and the catastrophe are far worse than he can be said to deserve, and others are engulfed in them who deserve such a fate less or not at all. Tragic terror is aroused in us because, though exceptional, he is sufficiently near to normal humankind for his fate to remind us of what can happen to human beings like ourselves, and because we see in it a combination of inexorable law and painful mystery. We recognise the principle of cause and effect where in a tragic world errors return upon those who make them, but we are also aware of the tragic disproportion between cause and effect. In a tragic world you may kick a stone and start an avalanche which will destroy you and others with you. Tragic pity is aroused in us by this disproportionate suffering, and also by all the kinds of suffering undergone by every character who has won our imaginative sympathy. Imaginative sympathy is wider than moral approval, and is felt even if suffering does seem a just and logical out- come. In addition to pity and terror we have a sense of tragic waste because catastrophe has affected so much that was great and fine. Yet we feel also a tragic exaltation. To our grief the men and women who represented those values have been destroyed, but the values themselves have been shown not to depend upon success, nor upon immunity from the worst of tragic suffering and disaster.

Comedies have been of two main kinds, or cross-bred from the two. In critical comedies the governing aim is to bring out the absurdity or irration- ality of follies and abuses, and make us laugh at them. Shakespeare's comedies often do this, but most of them belong primarily to the other kind – romantic comedy. Part of the romantic appeal is to our liking for suspense; they are dramas of averted threat, beginning in trouble and end- ing in joy. They appeal to the romantic senses of adventure and of wonder, and to complain that they are improbable is silly because the improbability, the marvellousness, is part of the pleasure. They dramatise stories of romantic love, accompanied by love doctrine – ideas and ideals of love. But they are plays in two tones, they are comic as well as romantic. There is often something to laugh at even in the love stories of the nobility and gentry, and just as there is high comedy in such incidents as the cross-purposes of the young Athenians in the wood, and Rosalind as 'Ganymede' teasing Orlando, there is always broad comedy for characters of lower rank. Even where one of the sub-plots has no effect on the main plot, it may take up a topic from it and present it in a more comic way.

What is there in the play to make us laugh or smile? We can distinguish many kinds of comedy it may employ. *Language* can amuse by its wit, or by absurdity, as in Bottom's malapropisms. Feste's nonsense-phrases, so fatuously admired by Sir Andrew, are deliberate, while his catechising of Olivia is clown-routine. Ass-headed Bottom embraced by the Fairy Queen is a *comic spectacle* combining costume and stage-business. His wanting to play every part is *comedy of character*. Phebe disdaining Silvius and in love with 'Ganymede', or Malvolio treating Olivia as though she had written him a love-letter is *comedy of situation*; the situation is laughably different from what Phebe or Malvolio supposes. A comic let-down or anticlimax can be devastating, as we see when Aragon, sure that he deserves Portia, chooses the silver casket only to find the portrait not of her but of a 'blinking idiot'. By *slapstick*, *caricature* or sheer *ridiculousness of situation*, comedy can be exaggerated into farce, which Shakespeare knows how to use on occasion. At the opposite extreme, before he averts the threat, he can carry it to the brink of tragedy, but always under control.

Dramatic irony is the result of a character or the audience anticipating an outcome which, comically or tragically, turns out very differently. Sometimes *we* foresee that it will. The speaker never foresees how ironical, looking back, the words or expectations will appear. When she says, 'A little water clears us of this deed' Lady Macbeth has no prevision of her sleep-walking words, 'Will these hands ne'er be clean?' There is irony in the way in which in all Shakespeare's tragic plays except *Richard II* comedy is found in the very heart of the tragedy. The Porter scene in *Macbeth* comes straight after Duncan's murder. In *Hamlet* and *Antony and Cleopatra* comic episodes lead into the catastrophe: the rustic Countryman brings Cleopatra the means of death, and the satirised Osric departs with Hamlet's assent to the fatal fencing match. The Porter, the Countryman and Osric are not mere 'comic relief', they contrast with the tragedy in a way that adds something to it, and affects our response.

A sense of the comic and the tragic is common ground between Shakespeare and his audience. Understandings shared with the audience are necessary to all drama. They include conventions, i.e. assumptions, contrary to what factual realism would demand, which the audience silently agrees to accept. It is, after all, by a convention, what Coleridge called a 'willing suspension of disbelief', that an actor is accepted as Hamlet. We should let a play teach us the conventions it depends on. Shakespeare's conventions allow him to take a good many liberties, and he never troubles about inconsistencies that wouldn't trouble an audience. What matters to the dramatist is the effect he creates. So long as we are responding as he would wish, Shakespeare would not care whether we could say by what means he has made us do so. But to appreciate his skill, and get a fuller understanding of his play, we have to distinguish these means, and find terms to describe them.

If you approach the Shakespeare play you are studying bearing in mind what is said to you here, then you will respond to it more fully than before. Yet like all works of artistic genius, Shakespeare's can only be analysed so far. His drama and its poetry will always have about them something 'which into words no critic can digest'.

HAROLD BROOKS

# ACKNOWLEDGEMENTS

Cover illustration: *Claudio and Isabella*, by William Holman Hunt, copyright Tate Gallery Publications Department.

# 1 INTRODUCTION

## 1.1  A PROBLEM PLAY

In the years 1602-4, Shakespeare wrote three comedies which are often grouped together under the title 'problem plays': *All's Well That Ends Well*, *Troilus and Cressida* and *Measure for Measure*. Shakespeare's comedies had already begun to grow darker, with plays like *Much Ado About Nothing* (c.1598) and *Twelfth Night* (c.1600) having sombre elements which are less in evidence in the earlier comedies. The problem plays coincide with the middle of the period in which the great tragedies were written: *Hamlet* (1600), *Othello* (?1603), *King Lear* (1605) and *Macbeth* (1606). The theory often advanced is that Shakespeare moved out of the gaiety of his earlier work in the 1590s into a more sombre drama, in which even the comedies have lost their lightness of touch. The three plays are sometimes labelled as tragicomedies. One of Shakespeare's contemporaries, John Fletcher, gave a rather superficial definition of this genre, but it certainly fits the 'problem' comedies: 'it wants [i.e. lacks] death which is enough to make it no tragedy, yet it brings some near to it which is enough to make it no comedy'.

Especially in the last hundred years, there has been unease at such a combination of frivolous and sombre elements. We are perplexed at seeing sexual banter disrupted by the threat of an imminent execution, or finding the comic trial scene with Elbow and Froth immediately followed by the moral seriousness of the Angelo-Isabella interviews. In one sense, therefore, the 'problem' is no more than a change in literary taste. Tragi-comedy is not as congenial to modern tastes as it seems to have been to Shakespeare's contemporaries.

But the problem goes deeper. Critics have identified in these plays a strong sense of cynicism, despair and even disgust at life. We see this, for example, in the Duke's almost nihilistic speech, 'Be absolute for death . . .' (III.i.5-41), and in his contemptuous reprimand to Pompey:

> Fie, sirrah, a bawd, a wicked bawd.
> The evil that thou causest to be done,
> That is thy means to live. Do thou but think
> What 'tis to cram a maw or clothe a back
> From such a filthy vice. Say to thyself,
> From their abominable and beastly touches
> I drink, I eat, array myself, and live.  (III.ii.18-24)

Indeed, none of the characters (including those who would chastise others, such as Angelo, Isabella and the Duke) is really likeable or possessed of a sympathetic warmth.

However, the cynicism of the play should not be exaggerated. For example, although Lucio and the brothel-keepers are condemned there is also an element of amused indulgence in their treatment. Lucio may be a whoring, treacherous fellow, full of slanders, but the comic elements in his speeches make our stern attitudes soften. The dénouement also offers at least some hope. Three marriages are arranged (the traditional number in Shakespearean comedy) and only Lucio's promises to be loveless. Above all, mercy is exercised by Mariana, Isabella and the Duke, and this illustrates that human goodness can transcend whatever weakness we all possess. The play is, to a great extent, a record of error and evil, but it does have positive notes. *Measure for Measure* is neither wholly cynical nor wholly joyful but an unsettling combination of both.

The 'problem' is therefore one of mode (comic or tragic?) and mood (cynical or not?) but it is also one of moral. What, precisely, is the play saying? This is perhaps the most fundamental question of all, and one we shall try to tackle in the pages that follow. It is enough for the moment to register the fact that widespread uncertainty on this point characterises the responses of critics, audiences and readers of *Measure for Measure*; an uncertainty not found to anything like the same degree in plays that one can confidently label either comic or tragic: *Othello*, *Julius Caesar*, *As You Like It* and *Much Ado About Nothing*.

## 1.2  INCONSISTENCIES

No other play by Shakespeare contains so many inconsistencies in the treatment of themes and characters as does *Measure for Measure*. The Duke steps down from his office in favour of Angelo in order that Vienna's 'strict statutes and most biting laws' (I.iii.19) be enforced severely, yet his actions in the final scene represent the triumph of leniency. His interview with Juliet (II.iii) makes clear his condemnation of her and Claudio's sexual misdemeanour, yet he plans the 'bed-trick' which, in the eyes of the church, involves equally sinful behaviour. The puritanical Isabella, who would rather sacrifice her brother's life than her chastity, is also a willing accomplice in the 'bed-trick'. She too finds Claudio's offence with Juliet abhorrent and yet she has no qualms about Mariana substituting herself at the secret assignation with Angelo.

Lucio appears to have an insider's information about Vincentio's doings. He tells Isabella that the Duke's

> giving out were of an infinite distance
> from his true-meant design    (I.iv.54–5)

and he appears to know that the Duke has disguised himself as a friar when he complains that it was mad of the Duke to 'usurp the beggary he was never born to' (III.ii.90). How has he come by this information? Nevill Coghill has suggested that Lucio knows that Friar Lodowick is the Duke in disguise, and that his slanders are meant as deliberate personal insults which, as Lucio knows, Vincentio cannot properly challenge without shedding his disguise. But there are two powerful arguments against the Coghill theory. The first is that nobody in Lucio's position would risk the extremely serious offence of slandering a prince to his face, or confiding to that prince his dealings with Mistress Kate Keepdown, knowing that punishment could well follow – as indeed it does. Secondly, Shakespeare's habit is to make important dramatic points very obvious; he has no tendency, nor any dramatic reason, for deliberate obscurity on such a point. It is always wiser to give credence to the obvious rather than the over-ingenious, and in this case common sense is against the Coghill theory. The debate about Lucio illustrates the kind of inconsistencies we find in the play.

In Shakespearean scholarship, one way of accounting for such inconsistencies is to devise an elaborate and ingenious 'reading' of the play which reconciles all the apparent anomalies into one unified and coherent whole. This approach is based on two errors. The first is the assumption that a Shakespeare play represents a perfectly succinct and unified view of its subject matter. If there appear to be internal contradictions, then we must, according to this theory, blame our own ignorance – of history, theology, contemporary politics, or whatever. Such a view fails to see the play as an entertainment written by an often hard-pressed and fallible playwright, who was routinely indifferent to the sort of consistency which we are discussing. The second error is to forget that what appear as anomalies in a play which we pore over week after week in a study hardly occur to a theatre audience which sees the play once. This audience concentrates its attention on what Shakespeare wants it to concentrate on and the niceties of consistency are rarely noticed.

In addition to these inconsistencies in theme and character portrayal, we also find factual inconsistencies. For example, Mistress Overdone announces the arrest of Claudio (I.ii.56-7) and gives the reason for it: 'it is for getting Madam Julietta with child' (66-7). Almost immediately, however, when alone with Pompey, the latter tells her that Claudio is 'carried to prison' (79) and she asks: 'But what's his offence?' (82) There is the usual ingenious critical explanation – Mary Lascelles believes that they are not talking about Claudio at all, but about someone else seen at a distance – but it is unconvincing.

There are a host of such irregularities in IV.iii. Vincentio says that he will write letters to Angelo and give them to the Provost to deliver; but the Provost comes and goes without any letter being written. Lucio's 'Good even' (148) is difficult to reconcile with the fact that it is clearly morning. The Duke's decision to meet Angelo

> at the consecrate fount
> A league below the city    (97-8)

is inexplicably changed to a meeting at the city gates. J. W. Lever, commenting on these factual anomalies, remarks that they are 'compatible with the oversights, hesitations, and changes of plan normal to a writer in the course of composition'. We also have to consider the strong possibility of textual corruption: this means that what Shakespeare originally wrote has become garbled or distorted in the process of transcribing and/or printing, as it passed through different hands.

Irregularities of detail are no more than irritating. But inconsistency in the presentation of themes and characters means that this play lacks a certain cohesion. Take, for example, the central issue of justice and mercy (further discussed under *Themes and Issues*). The play, in its early scenes, appears to be in favour of strict justice; but at the end it is clearly recommending mercy. Distinctions are made between private and public justice; private individuals are required to forgive wrongs done against them, whereas judges in the public judicial system need to protect the public good by punishing wrongdoers. But this distinction is further complicated by the fact that the play repeatedly stresses the need for judges to remember their own frail humanity and therefore to forgive. G. Wilson Knight wrote that such logical contradictions mirrored the illogic of religion itself. He refers to 'the sublime strangeness and unreason of Jesus' teaching'.

The best approach is to think of this play not as a logical and coherent statement, but as a work in which all kinds of irreconcilable ideas are thrown together as in a melting pot. Issues are raised, but the play does not always deal with them consistently.

## 1.3  JAMES I

Many of Vincentio's characteristics are almost certainly based on King James I (James VI of Scotland) who came to the English throne in 1603. (The play was probably written in the summer of 1604.) Some evidence for this assumption comes from a reading of James's work, *Basilikon Doron* (Greek for *The King's Gift*) which was published in Scotland in 1598. It was intended as a guide to kingship and the duties of a sovereign for his son, Prince Henry, and was on sale in England within days of Queen Elizabeth's death in 1603. Certain lines from Shakespeare's play closely echo passages from James's book. For example, the Duke's comment:

> Heaven doth with us as we with torches do,
> Not light them for themselves; for if our virtues
> Did not go forth of us, 'twere all alike
> As if we had them not    (I.i.32–5)

is close to the following sentiments:

> [Rulers should]  glister and shine before their people . . . that their persons as bright lamps of godliness and virtue may . . . give light to all their steps . . .

> it is not enough that ye have and retain (as prisoners) within yourself never so many good qualities and virtues, except that ye employ them, and set them on work . . .

However, we cannot be sure that Shakespeare was borrowing, because the notion of the necessity for displaying virtue is also found in well-known biblical passages. A third passage from James, a plea for moderation in government and the use of restraint in enforcing law, is practically a summary of the central moral of the play:

> make . . . temperance, queen of all the rest within you. I mean . . . that wise moderation, that first commanding yourself, shall as a queen, command all the affections and passions of your mind . . . even in your most virtuous actions, make ever moderation to be the chief ruler. For though holiness be the first and most requisite quality of a Christian, yet . . . moderate all your outward actions flowing therefrom. The like say I now of justice . . . For laws are ordained as rules of virtuous and social living, and not to be snares to trap your good subjects: and therefore the law must be interpreted according to the meaning, and not to the literal sense . . . And as I said of justice, so say I of clemency . . .

Vincentio's admission that "twas my fault to give the people scope' (I.iii.35) reflects James's admission in *Basilikon Doron* that he has ruled too laxly at the start of his Scottish reign. James's denunciation of those who slander princes is mirrored in Vincentio's anger on the same subject at III.ii.179–83 ('No might . . .') and IV.i.60–5 ('O place and greatness . . .').

Although these correspondences are striking, we need to be cautious in claiming with certainty that Shakespeare drew material directly from *Basilikon Doron*; this is because many of the king's ideas were common currency at the time and Shakespeare might well have come by them elsewhere.

Further possible evidence for the identification of the king with Vincentio is provided by James's behaviour. Just as Vincentio operates under a cloak of disguise, so James attempted (unsuccessfully) to remain incognito on a visit to the Exchange in March 1604 (a few months before the play was probably written) in order to watch the behaviour of the city's merchants. However, we must not make too much of this. The idea of rulers disguising themselves to go amongst the people is frequent in drama of the period. John Marston's *The Malcontent*, Thomas Middleton's *The Phoenix*, Samuel Rowley's *When You See Me You Know Me* (all 1604) and various anonymous plays all contain the theme.

More significant, for our purposes, is James's personal intervention in the criminal justice system. In April 1603, he presided as judge over a trial in Newark. On this occasion one thief was sentenced to death, but at the same time other prisoners were pardoned. Justice and mercy were thus both displayed, as they are in the play. Some months later, with a taste for a sudden theatrical effect, James ordered a reprieve from the death sentence for a group of traitors awaiting execution at Winchester. The reprieve was deliberately produced only at the very last moment, when the condemned were actually on the scaffold. Cynics are probably correct in assuming that the king's motive was to enhance his reputation as a merciful ruler for, viewed as a public relations exercise, it was a massive success. The Winchester crowds shouted with delight at James's clemency, and 'God Save the King' was proclaimed from every mouth. The suddenness and theatricality are closely echoed in Vincentio's own conduct of affairs in the final scene of *Measure for Measure*, and the last minute reprieve theme also appears in the play in connection with Barnardine's execution at IV.ii.148–50 ('We have very oft awaked him . . .').

James liked to cultivate the image of himself as a person of sombre and scholarly disposition. His demeanour at the Hampton Court conference prompted one commentator to describe him as 'a living library and a walking study'. There is perhaps a slight echo of this in Vincentio's claim that he has

> ever lov'd the life remov'd,
> And held in idle price to haunt assemblies,
> Where youth, and cost, witless bravery keeps.     (I.iii.8–10)

The final piece of evidence for connecting Vincentio with James is persuasive. News of the king's would-be secret visit to the Exchange leaked out. Noisy crowds pressed close to the royal party, causing James considerable distress. A contemporary tract, Gilbert Dugdale's *The Time Triumphant*, has a description of the incident. It includes the following remark:

> . . . will you in love press upon your sovereign thereby to offend him, your sovereign perchance mistake your love and punish it as an offence . . .

There are close parallels here with Angelo's comments in Act II:

> So play the foolish throngs with one that swounds,
> Come all to help him, and so stop the air
> By which he should revive; and even so
> The general subject to a well-wish'd king
> Quit their own part, and in obsequious fondness
> Crowd to his presence, where their untaught love
> Must needs appear offence.   (II.iv.24–30)

Although the lines are given to Angelo rather than Vincentio, it is widely thought that Shakespeare was nevertheless making a specific reference here to the king. A corroborating passage occurs in the play's opening scene, in which the Duke says:

> I love the people,
> But do not like to stage me to their eyes:
> Though it do well, I do not relish well
> Their loud applause and *Aves* vehement;
> Nor do I think the man of safe discretion
> That does affect it.   (I.i.67–72)

There is no historical evidence that James disliked crowds as such – quite the reverse. What appears to have happened is that Shakespeare seized on a particular topical incident – the royal visit to the Exchange – and referred to it indirectly through the characters of both the Duke and Angelo.

Shakespeare drew on James's ideas and behaviour because it was useful source material for his drama; but he probably had a second motive: flattery. His *Macbeth* (c.1606) also contains lightly-veiled praise of the monarch. A major reason for this praise was that James, on his accession, had taken over the patronage of Shakespeare's own acting company. The Lord Chamberlain's Men became The King's Men. Any dramatist would want to stay in favour with the man who was so useful to the company.

Vincentio is not meant as an exact portrait of the king – especially as Shakespeare's Duke has certain characteristics which are hardly praiseworthy. The most we can say is that certain aspects of Vincentio echo, in varying degrees of directness, some aspects of James's own life and thought.

## 1.4 BIBLICAL INFLUENCES

No other Shakespearean play is so strongly rooted in biblical teaching as *Measure for Measure*. The majority of the play's references are to Christ's Sermon on the Mount (St Matthew, chs. 5–7). The title itself, which stresses the importance of the theme of judgement, comes from this source:

> Judge not, that ye be not judged. For with what judgement ye judge, ye shall be judged; and with what measure ye mete, it shall be measured to you again.   (7:1)

There is an irony in the play's title because it clearly suggests that the plot will ensure punishment for those who dare to judge; and yet Angelo, the chief culprit, receives nothing like measure for measure.

I have chosen here two representative passages. It should of course always be borne in mind that the biblical influence is not merely a question of certain speeches in the play having similarities with Bible passages; the entire work, in its structure and moral conception, is profoundly Christian. I have endeavoured to make that abundantly clear in the detailed discussions of the play throughout this book. The first passage occurs in the opening scene:

> DUKE                    Angelo:
> There is a kind of character in thy life
> That to th'observer doth thy history
> Fully unfold. Thyself and thy belongings
> Are not thine own so proper as to waste
> Thyself upon thy virtues, they on thee.
> Heaven doth with us as we with torches do,
> Not light them for themselves; for if our virtues
> Did not go forth of us, 'twere all alike
> As if we had them not. Spirits are not finely touch'd
> But to fine issues;   (I.i.26–36)

There are at least three New Testament passages evoked here. The first comes from the Sermon on the Mount:

> Ye are the light of the world. A city that is set on an hill cannot be hid. Neither do men light a candle, and put it under a bushel, but on a candlestick; and it giveth light unto all that are in the house. Let your light so shine before men that they may see your good works, and glorify your Father which is in heaven.   (St Matthew, 5:14–16)

There is a certain irony in Shakespeare's evoking this famous sermon in so far as it also contains other injunctions having a direct bearing on other aspects of the play. Earlier in the sermon, Christ says:

Blessed are they which do hunger and thirst after righteousness . . .
Blessed are the merciful, for they shall obtain mercy.   (6-7)

Angelo is soon to fail on both counts.

There are also close parallels to Luke's gospel, 8:43-46. The Duke's 'issues', 'touch'd' and 'go forth of us' echo Luke's 'issue', 'touched' and 'virtue is gone out of me'. Angelo becomes associated in our minds with Christ himself.

Luke 8:16 contains Christ's insistence that candles must not be hidden under beds, but placed in candlesticks. The very next verse (17) contains a remark which is prophetic of what happens in Shakespeare's play: 'For nothing is secret, that shall not be made manifest: neither any thing hid, that shall not be known and come abroad.' It has been argued that at the very moment of hearing Angelo compared to a candle of virtue, audiences familiar with this New Testament passage would have in their minds the related promise that secrets would be revealed; this in turn might give rise to the suspicion that perhaps there is something hidden about Angelo which in time will be disclosed.

The second extract from the play to be examined here occurs at the end of the Duke's conversation with the Provost in IV.ii, when Vincentio observes:

Look, th'unfolding star calls up the shepherd. Put not yourself into amazement how these things should be; all difficulties are but easy when they are known.   (IV.ii.202-5)

The joint evocation of 'star', 'shepherd', and the idea of amazement has a very strong resonance of the Nativity. One would not want to go so far as to say that, as a subject, the Nativity has any special relevance to the passage. Rather, it simply shows how New Testament language, whether or not by deliberate design, permeates the words of the play – and especially the words of the Duke. The rest of the passage is very similar to Luke 8:17 quoted above ('For nothing is secret . . .'. This is also found in a slightly different version in Matthew, 10:26). In speaking such language, the Duke becomes associated in our minds with something holy, if not actually divine.

It is not surprising that biblical echoes should assume such prominence in the play. After all, so much of what happens in the story is of an overtly religious nature. Isabella is about to enter a convent, the Duke disguises himself as a friar and frequently speaks in a religious capacity, and one of the starting points of the plot, Claudio's offence of fornication, is traditionally far more a matter for religious than secular intervention. Additionally, one constantly finds parcels of Christian teaching paraphrased in different parts of the text. The Duke's comments to Claudio throughout the prison scene (III.i) are often of this type, and Isabella provides perhaps the best example, giving to Angelo a moving statement of the doctrine of salvation:

> Alas, alas!
> Why, all the souls that were, were forfeit once,
> And He that might the vantage best have took
> Found out the remedy. How would you be
> If He, which is the top of judgement, should
> But judge you as you are? O, think on that,
> And mercy then will breathe within your lips,
> Like man new made.   (II.ii.72-9)

# 2 SYNOPSIS

Vincentio, Duke of Vienna, announces suddenly that he must leave the city at once. He appoints Angelo to take his place, although admitting that the more senior Escalus should, by rights, have been selected.

We are now introduced to Lucio and his associates, who are amusing themselves with bawdy joking. They are distracted by the news that Angelo, the new deputy, has condemned to death one of Lucio's friends, Claudio. His offence is making his friend Juliet pregnant. At the same time, Angelo has decreed that all the brothels in the suburbs be demolished.

Claudio enters, led through the streets by his gaoler, and tells Lucio his plight. He asks Lucio to visit his sister Isabella in her nunnery and persuade her to help him.

We now discover that Vincentio is not really in Poland, as he had let it be thought, but still in Vienna. He explains to Friar Thomas the reason for the subterfuge: Vienna has strict laws, but as Duke, he has culpably failed to enforce them; now they are openly flouted. Angelo has been appointed to make the law respected again. The Duke disguises himself as a friar so that he can observe Angelo's conduct.

Lucio visits Isabella in the nunnery, and she agrees to help her brother. Meanwhile, Escalus tries unsuccessfully to convince Angelo that the death sentence passed on Claudio is too severe. The two men then act as judges in a hilariously complicated case brought by the dim Constable Elbow against Pompey, a brothel-keeper, and his friend Froth. Angelo, exasperated by their evasions, leaves the hearing to Escalus, who shows his merciful nature by releasing both men with merely a warning.

Isabella visits Angelo and pleads for her brother's life. As she warms to her theme, Angelo finds himself sexually aroused by her virtue. He tells her to return the next day. She departs, and in a soliloquy he expresses moral revulsion at the discovery of his own lust.

Isabella returns next day, and Angelo – after a series of mostly oblique hints which confuse her – openly tells her that Claudio will die unless she surrenders her body to him. Isabella is horrified and threatens to denounce him publicly. Angelo tells her that nobody would believe her, and exits. Alone, Isabella decides to preserve her chastity rather than Claudio's life.

At the prison, the disguised Duke consoles Claudio by arguing that what he is losing – life – is not worth the having. Isabella arrives and reveals Angelo's demand to her brother. At first, Claudio is firm that his own death is preferable to his sister's shame, but gradually his fear of death makes him plead with her to give in to Angelo. Isabella responds with almost hysterical anger. Vincentio, who has overheard everything, intervenes and reveals to Isabella a way of saving Claudio and satisfying Angelo. Isabella is to pretend to agree to the deputy's plan, but another woman – Mariana, originally betrothed to Angelo but thrown off by him when her dowry was lost at sea – will take her place at the assignation. Then, when the truth comes to light, Angelo will be forced to marry the woman he wronged. Claudio is not told of the plan and still believes that he is to die.

The Duke meets Pompey being taken to prison and strongly denounces his bawd's trade. Lucio enters, and refuses Pompey help with bail. He is then left alone with the disguised Duke, and, pretending to be an intimate of Vincentio's, describes the latter as lascivious, often drunk and stupid. The Duke tells Lucio that he will have to justify his remarks later.

Isabella and the Duke visit Mariana and persuade her to agree to the 'bed-trick'. Vincentio then goes to the prison, expecting the arrival of Claudio's pardon. Instead, Angelo has ordered that the execution take place even sooner than planned, and Claudio's head be sent to him as evidence that his orders have been obeyed. Vincentio convinces the reluctant Provost to execute another prisoner, Barnardine, and substitute his head. However, Barnardine is drunk and insists on more time to prepare himself for death. Vincentio agrees that, if executed now, Barnardine's soul would be damned. They decide, instead, to send Angelo the head of Ragozine, a pirate who died in the prison that morning. Isabella enters, and the Duke pretends Claudio is already dead. Angelo and Escalus have, meanwhile, been instructed to meet the returning Duke at the city gates, where the play's final scene takes place.

No longer in disguise, Vincentio is welcomed home. Isabella steps forward from the crowd and denounces Angelo, claiming that he has slept with her. Angelo tells the Duke that she must be insane. The Duke orders her arrest. Then Mariana comes forward and contradicts Isabella, saying that it was she who slept with Angelo. The latter not only pretends innocence, but asks the Duke's permission to punish both women. Vincentio agrees and exits, returning almost immediately in his friar's guise. He says that the Duke must be unjust to have left Isabella to be judged by the very man she accuses. Escalus becomes angry at this and orders him to be imprisoned. In the ensuing scuffle, Lucio pulls off his friar's hood, and the Duke's true identity is revealed.

Angelo confesses immediately and asks for death. Vincentio orders him to wed Mariana. He does so, and returns. Vincentio then sentences him to death. Mariana pleads for his life, unsuccessfully; she begs Isabella to plead with her. Isabella does so, even though she still believes Claudio dead. Only at this stage does the Duke order Claudio to be produced. He is pardoned, as is Barnardine. Vincentio proposes marriage to Isabella. Angelo is reprieved from death and Lucio forced to marry the prostitute whom he made pregnant.

# 3 SUMMARY AND CRITICAL COMMENTARY

### Act I, Scene i

*Summary*

The Duke announces that Angelo will act as his deputy while he is absent from Vienna. He exits, leaving Angelo and Escalus to discuss the various powers that they have each been given, and which are set out in their written commissions.

*Commentary*

The play opens with the Duke's speech in praise of Escalus. Vincentio describes his assistant not merely as knowledgeable, but as superior even to himself in the science of government. For the audience, it is therefore very odd indeed that he should immediately follow this praise of Escalus with the announcement that it is Angelo, not the 'ancient Lord' (as the *dramatis personae* calls him) who is to be appointed deputy. The obvious and expected choice is neglected, and we have to wait until Scene iii to discover the Duke's reasons for his apparently wayward choice.

Angelo's first appearance is immediately preceded by strong praise from Escalus:

> If any in Vienna be of worth
> To undergo such ample grace and honour,
> It is Lord Angelo.   (22-4)

The fact that even someone as experienced and wise as Escalus can badly misjudge a man prepares us for the play's emphasis on deceptive outward appearances and 'seeming'.

Angelo then addresses the Duke:

> Always obedient to your Grace's will,
> I come to know your pleasure.   (25-6)

Already we can detect an elaborate formality which suggests the cold austere man, the Puritan. There is, too, a combination of excessive deference and self-esteem in the first of the lines which squares with what we are to see of Angelo's character later.

The Duke now delivers a speech of high commendation. Angelo is compared to a torch which should not be hidden away, but placed in public prominence so that its light will not be wasted. The fact that this figure of speech is based on famous New Testament passages (see 1.4: Biblical Influences) makes a clear connection between Angelo and holiness, a connection reinforced by his very name.

Angelo's reply to the praise is usually taken to be an attempt to refuse the office:

> Now, good my lord,
> Let there be some more test made of my metal,
> Before so noble and so great a figure
> Be stamp'd upon it.   (47–50)

However, it is possible that Angelo is merely employing a polite but not truly sincere self-deprecation; he knows perfectly well that the Duke has made up his mind about the appointment and has no intention of changing it.

The Duke's reply, brushing aside Angelo's objection, contains a key to his whole character. He announces that his departure has to be sudden – so much so that 'Matters of needful value' (55) have to be neglected. One of the consequences of this is that, the Duke having departed, Escalus and Angelo are rather confused as to their respective duties. As Vincentio's declared purposes do not seem to require suddenness to be effective, this lack of planning is in line with his conduct in neglecting the laws of Vienna.

## Act I, Scene ii

*Summary*
Lucio and his friends are engaged in conversation. They begin with comments on international affairs and move on to general banter, especially jocular references to venereal disease. Mistress Overdone, a brothel-keeper, enters and tells them that Claudio has been arrested for making Juliet pregnant, and that he is to be executed for it.

Pompey enters and tells Overdone that there is a proclamation by which all the brothels in the suburbs are to be demolished. Claudio enters, being led through the streets for the purpose of public humiliation. He explains his situation to his friend Lucio, at first seeming to accept the justice of his punishment, but then saying that it is very severe. He asks

Lucio to visit his sister Isabella, a novice about to take her vows and enter a convent, in order that she might help him by approaching Angelo. Lucio agrees.

*Commentary*

After the ponderous, formal exchanges of the previous scene, Shakespeare, with his typical love of contrast, now plunges us into a world of brothel frequenters, engaged in witty puns about politics, religion and venereal disease.

The contrast of the scenes is not merely a theatrical device to provide us with greater variety. It emphasises the gap between the fine, high-sounding words of the rulers and the earthy attitudes of the ruled.

When Claudio enters, Angelo's severity is made apparent by the fact that not only is Claudio condemned to death, but he is subjected to the humiliation of being paraded through the streets as a spectacle. However, Angelo's 'commission' from the Duke must surely include clear instructions on the tightening up of the law, which is one of the two reasons that the Duke has appointed him as deputy. (See discussion of I.iii, below). He wants Angelo to 'strike home' (I.iii.41) in his name. The resulting severity can therefore largely be imputed to Angelo's obedience to Vincentio, as well as to excessive zeal or natural harshness. With this in mind, it is surely ironic that, later in the scene, Lucio suggests that Claudio should 'Send after the Duke, and appeal to him' (163-4).

Claudio's attitude to his offence is curious. At first, he seems to imply acceptance even of the death penalty: 'yet still 'tis just' (115). He accuses himself of 'too much liberty' (117), of having pursued 'A thirsty evil' (122). Even to tell Lucio the details of his crime 'would offend again' (128). However, immediately after this, his attitude changes to that of complaint against the unreasonableness of the proceedings against him. Juliet is 'fast my wife' (136) and his only failure has been neglecting to go through the religious ceremony. (We note in passing that Claudio's reason for delaying the ceremony is to make certain of the payment of a dowry. This links his marriage with the betrothal of Angelo and Mariana, which the former breaks off when a dowry is lost at sea.)

One of the reasons Claudio particularly wants his sister to speak for him is that:

> she hath prosperous art
> When she will play with reason and discourse   (174-5)

The use of the word 'art', suggesting as it then did the crafty and the underhand, with the word 'play', gives an overall impression that Isabella is liable to say whatever is expedient to an argument, whether it is true or not. We are to see this characteristic in the two interviews with Angelo (II.ii; II.iv).

## Act I, Scene iii

### Summary

The Duke explains to Friar Thomas why he wishes to remain in Vienna secretly, seeking the disguise of a friar. For fourteen years he has neglected to enforce the strict laws of the state, so that now they are openly flouted. He did not feel able to correct the situation himself, as he was the man responsible for the neglect in the first place. He also wishes to avoid the slander inevitably attaching to a severe ruler. He has therefore appointed Angelo to enforce the laws in his stead. He concludes by saying of Angelo that he is outwardly puritanical, but that once he has power, his character might change.

### Commentary

One of Shakespeare's favourite devices is to start a scene in the middle of an exchange. The first thing we hear is a reply and we have to infer the original remark. The technique draws us straight away into the dialogue, seizing our attention and creating a sense of immediacy. (In *Hamlet* and *Othello*, Shakespeare does this at the very beginning of the play. There is another good example in *Measure for Measure* at III.i.)

Here, the Duke is rebutting a previous suggestion from the friar that it is some love intrigue that is prompting him to disguise himself. These two themes – disguise and love – figure prominently in the play. Vincentio's boast that his 'complete bosom' (3) is strong enough to withstand 'the dribbling dart of love' (2) is shown to be false, for somewhere along the line he falls in love with Isabella, and offers to marry her at the end of the play. His pretending to be a friar is part of the play's exploration of 'seeming' – whether people really are what they appear to be. As Vincentio asks himself at the end of the scene whether Angelo will truly turn out to be as 'precise' as he seems (50-4), it is clearly ironic that he himself should so clearly be a 'seemer'; and not only in his disguise. Throughout the play he tells lie after lie in order to advance his schemes, culminating in the play's final scene in which he deliberately misleads almost everyone about almost everything. Clearly, his 'seeming' is not as base as Angelo's but aspects of it – particularly his pretending to Isabella that her brother is dead – have been found by many critics to be unacceptably cruel.

Once he has listened to the Duke's reasons for appointing a deputy, Friar Thomas wonders why he has not attempted to enforce the law himself. Vincentio gives two reasons. The first is as follows:

> Sith 'twas my fault to give the people scope,
> 'Twould be my tyranny to stike and gall them (35-6)

He is disqualifying himself from a public judicial function on grounds of personal unfitness and this raises the very question at issue when Angelo later abuses the same judicial office.

The second reason the Duke gives does him little credit:

> I have on Angelo impos'd the office;
> Who may in th'ambush of my name strike home,
> And yet my nature never in the fight
> To do it slander (40-3)

The last phrase is thought to be textually corrupt (that is, what Shakespeare originally wrote has been garbled in the process of copying and printing) but the gist of the passage is clear: Angelo can do the Duke's dirty work for him and attract to himself all the subsequent unpopularity whilst the Duke's name will remain free of slander. This is not the only occasion on which the Duke attaches what appears to be excessive importance to his public reputation. (See III.ii.179-83; 224-30; IV.i.60-5.)

It is clear, then, why he appoints a deputy; but why Angelo rather than Escalus? Not only do we know that he reveres Escalus's wisdom and learning (I.i.3-13); we also know that he suspects that Angelo is less virtuous than he seems. This is apparent both from his knowledge of Angelo's disgraceful treatment of Mariana (III.i.212-30) and his expectation that Angelo may well change when in power:

> Hence shall we see
> If power change purpose, what our seemer be.   (53-4)

There are two reasons why Angelo is appointed despite this. The first is that Escalus is too lenient a judge to suit the Duke's purpose of enforcing 'strict statutes and most biting laws' (19). His leniency is all too apparent when, for example, he hears the case of constable Elbow against Pompey Bum (II.i). Escalus's kind-heartedness would obviously be just as disastrous as the Duke's own total neglect of the law has been. Angelo is chosen because the Duke knows that he will be severe. The second reason for choosing Angelo is that the Duke has noticed that he is very cold and morally strict and Vincentio wishes to set up a test to see whether power will corrupt him.

Whereas the desire to install a strict deputy is a matter of public policy, the desire to test an individual - especially in the capacity of a judge, where the testing is likely, as in this case, to prove a danger to others - seems like an irresponsible personal whim. Critics have suggested three ways out of this difficulty. One is to argue that Vincentio is not testing Angelo at all, or at least not until he overhears the truth of his deputy's evil. When he says:

> Hence shall we see
> If power change purpose, what our seemers be   (53-4)

he is merely voicing a fear in the back of his mind, rather than an expectation. A second approach is to see in the Duke an all-powerful, virtuous
God-like figure who moves benevolently behind the scenes ensuring that
mishaps and disasters are averted and that honest government is restored
to Vienna. This is to a certain extent true of what happens during the play,
but we have already discussed certain aspects of Vincentio's character
which make him seem far from God-like.

The third approach applies not merely to the character of the Duke but
to all the many inconsistencies in this, and other Shakespearean plays. In
this approach we do not necessarily see all characters as fixed, logical or
psychologically convincing, or seek to explain their behaviour with reference
to only one theory or interpretation. That is to say, we learn to accept and
to ignore inconsistencies. (For further discussion, see 1.2: 'Inconsistencies'.)


## Act I, Scene iv

*Summary*
Isabella remarks to the nun Francisca that she would prefer to see the
regulations governing convent life more strict. Lucio enters and tells her of
Claudio's predicament. At first she does not believe him, and later doubts
whether her intervention would have any good effect. However, after some
encouragement, she agrees to do what she can.


*Commentary*
Isabella's first words in the play are a complaint that the regulations of the
nunnery are too lax. As the Poor Clares were well-known for the strictness
of their Rule, her attitude immediately links her in our minds with Angelo.
Both of them are embarking on a new episode in their lives, and both have
something of the fanaticism of the novice. There is also a certain naïvety
about her. When Lucio announces the reason for his visit, she is so un-
worldly that she simply does not believe it possible: 'Sir, make me not
your story' (30).

The rich comedy of the rakish Lucio visiting a nunnery is sometimes
missed in reading the play, but is apparent in the theatre, where ironic
intonations and stage movement will suggest the disparity in the two
characters' attitude to Claudio's deed. The flippant mockery of Lucio's
address,

> Hail virgin, if you be – as those cheek-roses
> Proclaim you are no less   (16–17)

has no malice in it. He cannot resist the temptation to rally the austere
novice:

> I hold you as a thing enskied and sainted
> By your renouncement, an immortal spirit,
> And to be talk'd with in sincerity,
> As with a saint.   (34-7)

Isabella's frosty reply: 'You do blaspheme the good, in mocking me' (38) is rather self-important, and Lucio is egged on to a comically metaphorical description of the sexual coupling of Juliet and Claudio.

Lucio's account of Angelo's character and attitude to the law is embellished by witty images: Angelo's blood is 'very snow-broth' (58); libertines:

> have for long run by the hideous law
> As mice by lions . . .   (63-4)

These images stress the humour of the scene and often have the effect of endearing Lucio to the audience.

The two opposites, liberty and restraint, are central terms in the moral world of the play. We have seen examples of excessive liberty in Claudio and Lucio, and now we hear of a man of personal restraint: Angelo is a man who

> doth rebate and blunt his natural edge
> With profits of the mind, study and fast.   (60-61)

Lucio's long-windedness (49-71) is contrasted with Isabella's abrupt reply; she is not one for frivolous word-play. Her question: 'Doth he so/ Seek his life?' (71-2) not only has a terseness which strengthens the feeling of sincerity that we have, but it is expressed in words which make Angelo's legal decision sound like a personal vendetta. It is one of the many occasions in the play when the personal and public aspects of legal justice are implicitly contrasted.

Isabella is at first wholly lacking in confidence when she is asked to intercede for her brother:

> Alas, what poor ability's in me
> To do him good!   (75-6)

It is thanks to Lucio's insistent encouragement, both here and at II.ii, that Claudio's execution is postponed. Lucio thus acts as a true friend to Claudio.

## Act II, Scene i

*Summary*
Angelo and Escalus are discussing Claudio's case. Angelo's view is that only if justice is strict will the law be respected. Escalus argues that justice

should be mild; he urges Angelo to consider the workings of his own affections.

Constable Elbow enters with two defendants, Froth and Pompey, and presents them before Angelo and Escalus, who are to act as judges. Elbow is stupid and his case against the two is hopelessly garbled. Impatiently, Angelo leaves the court while the hearing is still in progress, leaving the matter wholly to Escalus. The latter is lenient and releases both men with only a warning.

*Commentary*
This scene shows us Escalus as a merciful judge. Discussing Claudio's sentence, Angelo tells his fellow justice that strictness is necessary:

> We must not make a scarecrow of the law,
> Setting it up to fear the birds of prey,
> And let it keep one shape till custom make it
> Their perch, and not their terror.   (1-4)

The words are a clear echo of the Duke's at I.iii.23–31. Escalus, however, wants justice to be tempered with mercy:

> Let us be keen, and rather cut a little,
> Than fall, and bruise to death.   (5-6)

Escalus's main point (one that Isabella herself makes twice, at II.ii.64-6, 137-42) is that Angelo should consider whether in his own past he might not have found himself in exactly the same situation as Claudio (8-16). This is an emotional appeal rather than an argument, and is easily demolished by Angelo. He stresses the difference between being tempted and actually giving in to that temptation. If there are guilty judges or jurymen, then the answer is to condemn them too, in due course, not to pardon the original accused. Implicit in this argument is the idea that a jury of fallible and even guilty human beings can nevertheless pass sentence on an offender without being unfair or unjust. Nowhere in the play is there a logical rebuttal of Angelo's wholly coherent stance towards justice as expressed in these lines (17-31). Even Escalus is hesitant about the value of mercy by the end of the scene, so that whilst he commiserates with Claudio's lot, it is based on feelings of pity rather than reasoned argument:

> Mercy is not itself, that oft looks so;
> Pardon is still the nurse of second woe.
> But yet, poor Claudio! There is no remedy.   (280-2)

The notion that *Measure for Measure* is a straightforward rejection of strict justice in favour of a softening mercy is a dangerous simplification.

With the entrance of Elbow, Froth and Pompey (40) we have a court scene which provides a comic view of justice, contrasting with the sombreness of Angelo's pronouncements on the law. Angelo is angry and impatient with the tedious and irrelevant evidence offered, and soon leaves:

> This will last out a night in Russia
> When nights are longest there. I'll take my leave,
> And leave you to the hearing of the cause;
> Hoping you'll find good cause to whip them all.   (133-6)

By contrast, Escalus is indulgent, releasing both Froth and Pompey with only a warning. His relaxed attitude also comes through in his joking manner. He pretends to find Pompey's defence of Froth - that the latter has a kind face and therefore cannot be guilty - legally satisfactory (158); and with heavy irony he tells Elbow that he is releasing Pompey, as though this were a severe punishment (182-5). He even indulges in quibbles on Pompey's bum (214-16) and his historical namesake's battles with Julius Caesar (244-6).

Notwithstanding all Elbow's ignorance, and Pompey's evasions and long-windedness, serious truths do surface in this scene. When Escalus asks Pompey if his bawd's trade is legal, he replies, 'If the law would allow it, sir' (224). The comic platitude stresses the serious point that nothing in the human world is fixed and immutable; that just as laws are made, so they can be repealed or neglected. In particular, the law on sexual conduct is unrealistically strict and not workable: 'Does your worship mean to geld and splay all the youth of the city?' (227-8) is Pompey's comment on the new clamp-down. In his view, this is the only way that prostitution will cease as a trade.

The absurd complexities of Pompey's story seem to provide a general comment on the impossibility of ever getting to the bottom of any question, or judging it perfectly.

## Act II, Scene ii

*Summary*
The Provost asks Angelo to confirm the order for Claudio's execution; Angelo does so, angered that the Provost should even have asked about the matter. Isabella is admitted, accompanied by Lucio, who urges her on from the sidelines throughout the scene. She pleads with Angelo to spare Claudio's life, using a wide variety of arguments and becoming increasingly angry and emotionally involved as the scene proceeds. Angelo is stubborn and holds out for a time, but at some point he becomes aware that he is sexually attracted to Isabella on account of her virtuous behaviour. Without promising anything, he asks her to visit him again the next day.

*Commentary*

Once again, Angelo's severity is brought to our attention. His impatience with the Provost at the beginning of the scene is marvellously rendered in three consecutive rhetorical questions, no doubt delivered in a brisk staccato:

> Did I not tell thee yea? Hadst thou not order?
> Why dost thou ask again?   (8-9)

Angelo's personal coldness emerges in the way he deals with Juliet. She must no be indulged: 'Let her have needful, but not lavish means' (24). The pompous and legalistic description of her as 'the fornicatress' (23) contrasts with the Provost's phrase 'the groaning Juliet' (15) which suggests solicitude.

Angelo is at first reluctant to see Isabella. Only when assured that she is 'a very virtuous maid' (20) does he say: 'Well, let her be admitted' (22). It is as if Angelo fears that his purity and virtue might be endangered by proximity to women. It is a crucial irony that he feels safer with a novice and a 'virtuous maid', little realising that it is precisely her virtues and purity which will be his undoing.

When Isabella enters, Angelo asks the Provost to remain behind, presumably to act as a witness and also to forestall any suggestion of impropriety which might arise were they to be left alone together.

Isabella's opening argument (29-33) has attracted much comment. Most critics assume that she does not know that Claudio is married to Juliet. Certainly, Lucio did not tell her in I.iv; on the other hand, many things in a Shakespeare play are assumed to have been said off-stage. At any rate, she clearly considers Claudio's offence very grievous. The effect is to emphasise the overly-pious and Puritanical part of her nature which we saw at her first appearance (I.iv.1-5).

The strength of Isabella's pleading does not always lie in the quality of her arguments. To say, for example, that Claudio's fault should be condemned but not Claudio himself (35-6) is not intellectually impressive, and Angelo refutes it easily. Similarly, her comparison of the killing of Claudio and the 'fowl of season' (85-8) is a ridiculous parallel. What is impressive in Isabella's pleading is its tenacity. Her obdurate refusal to be denied, once Lucio has given her heart, leads to a crescendo of anger. The plaintive 'Must he needs die?' (48) turns to the impertinent 'Too late? Why, no.' (57) and finally to the full-blooded contempt for what she sees as Angelo's abuse of his office. For her, he becomes

> . . . man, proud man,
> Dress'd in a little brief authority.   (118-19)

Then her anger softens, the tone becomes less strident; her last speech is a gentle offer to bribe him 'with true prayers' (152).

Perhaps Isabella's strongest point is her appeal to Angelo to imagine himself in Claudio's position:

> If he had been as you, and you as he,
> You would have slipp'd like him, but he like you
> Would not have been so stern.   (64-6)

We can gauge the importance of this point from the fact that it is so frequently made in the play. Escalus has already appealed to Angelo on these grounds at II.i.8-16 ('Let but your honour know . . .'), and Isabella comes back to it in this scene:

>                     . . . Go to your bosom,
> Knock there, and ask your heart what it doth know
> That's like my brother's fault. If it confess
> A natural guiltiness, such as is his,
> Let it not sound a thought upon your tongue
> Against my brother's life.   (137-42)

It is, of course, a marvellous irony, for at the very moment Isabella is speaking, Angelo is experiencing precisely that 'natural guiltiness' in relation to her.

In the first half of the interview, Angelo's reluctance to be convinced is rendered by the brevity of his remarks. Between lines 26 and 66, no fewer than seven of his speeches are of one line, five of them of only four words or less. For example:

> Well: what's your suit? (28)
>
> Well: the matter? (33)
>
> Maiden, no remedy. (48)
>
> I will not do't. (51)
>
> Pray you be gone. (66)

It is only when her pleas begin to have some effect that he is prepared to be more expansive.

Angelo presents a whole battery of arguments to fend off Isabella's persistence. For Shakespeare's contemporaries, however, the strongest weapon in his arsenal is his distinction between private and public wrong. He cannot be merciful as can a private individual, because he is a public upholder of law and has the responsibility to judge and punish like God himself: 'It is the law, not I, condemn your brother' (80). The injunction in the Sermon on the Mount to 'judge not' does not apply to him.

Another strong argument, altogether more sophisticated, emerges when Isabella pleads with him to 'show some pity' (100):

> I show it most of all when I show justice;
> For then I pity those I do not know,
> Which a dismiss'd offence would after gall,
> And do him right that, answering one foul wrong,
> Lives not to act another.  (101–5)

This is especially interesting because the whole scene seems to be posited on the view that justice and mercy are opposites. Indeed, critics often represent the play as a battle between these two concepts. But, here is Angelo making the point that strict justice can itself be a kind of mercy. Even the virtuous Escalus, who knows all about the 'properties' of 'government' (I.i.3) has already made the same point:

> Mercy is not itself, that oft looks so;
> Pardon is still the nurse of second woe.   (II.i.280–1)

Escalus's view turns out to be prophetic; the bawd whom he has just leniently released goes on to re-offend until his re-arrest in III.ii.

As she departs, Isabella tells Angelo: 'Heaven keep your honour safe' (158). She means 'honour' as a respectful title, but it ironically glances at the danger to Angelo's honour from this encounter. Lest we miss the pun, Shakespeare has it repeated four lines later.

Lucio's role in this scene is very sympathetic. We, like him, are on the sidelines rooting for Isabella, and his concern for Claudio appears to spring from genuine friendship. His nasty sneers at Pompey's arrest later (in III.ii) show us a less pleasant aspect of his character.

### Act II, Scene iii

*Summary*
The Duke visits the prison disguised as a friar; he is to retain this disguise in all his appearances in the play until IV.v. He sees Juliet and questions her about her attitude to her offence. She is genuinely contrite and not merely sorry because her sin has brought her shame.

*Commentary*
In introducing Juliet to the Duke, the Provost describes her as having 'blister'd her report' (12). Although the expression is figurative, it reminds us of the literal blistering or branding of the forehead to which prostitutes were subjected, and suggests that the Provost views her fornication as very serious. However, his attitude to Claudio is completely different. He is,

> More fit to do another such offence
> Than die for this.   (14–15)

echoing Lucio's comment to Isabella in the nunnery scene:

> . . . if myself might be his judge,
> He should receive his punishment in thanks.   (I.iv.27–8)

This application of a double standard in matters of sexual morality is shared by the Duke. When Juliet admits that the fornication was 'mutually committed' (27), his reply is: 'Then was your sin of heavier kind than his' (28).

The Duke's testing of Juliet's state of mind reminds us that, in the play as a whole, it is not merely Angelo who is subjected to some kind of test: the Provost, Escalus, Isabella and Juliet all undergo a similar process at Vincentio's hands.


## Act II, Scene iv

### Summary

In an opening soliloquy, Angelo speaks of himself as a hypocrite whose true character is hidden. He acknowledges the power that sexual desire has over him. Isabella enters and he tells her that Claudio must die. She makes to depart, so he detains her by promising that Claudio might be indefinitely reprieved. He asks her whether she would be prepared to surrender up her body in exchange for her brother's life. Isabella appears to misunderstand him, and there then begins a complex series of exchanges which alternate between bluntness and obscurity. It is only with dogged persistence that Angelo manages to convince Isabella that he is in earnest in his proposal. She threatens to denounce him unless he pardons her brother. He tells her that nobody will believe her story, and he repeats his demand and exits. In a concluding soliloquy, Isabella speaks of her brother as one who would not hesitate to die many times over rather than allow her to sacrifice her chastity. She also says that her chastity is more important than her brother's life.


### Commentary

On entering, Isabella comes straight to the point: 'I am come to know your pleasure' (31). Preoccupied by lustful anticipation, Angelo gloatingly takes up 'pleasure' in its sexual sense in an aside (32–3). When, with bluntness matching hers, he tells her that 'Your brother cannot live' (33) her reaction is the same as it was at II.ii.41–2: to give up. Making to depart, she once again wishes that 'Heaven keep your honour' (34) with the 'honour' pun that we saw earlier (II.ii.158; 162).

Angelo now realises he has mismanaged the preliminaries; Isabella is already going and it is essential for his purposes that she stay longer. He therefore tantalizes her with a hope that Claudio's execution can be postponed indefinitely. Then, ignoring her questioning about this possible 'reprieve' (39), he launches into a condemnation of sexual misbehaviour, which prompts Isabella to urge a gentler view: ' 'Tis set down so in heaven, but not in earth' (50). This appears to mean that, although God equally punishes the murderer and the fornicator, in human law the sexual offence is treated far more leniently. It is interesting to note here how Isabella, the pious novice, sides with the secular rather than the religious view of punishment.

This is exactly what Angelo wants to hear. If Isabella is now saying that fornication is not so odious after all, what better moment for Angelo to choose to offer her the terms of his foul bargain. In making his proposal, he seeks to make the hoped-for sexual encounter more acceptable to Isabella by softening his description of it. What had been 'filthy vices' (42) now become something almost attractive: 'sweet uncleanness' (54). Isabella appears not to understand him, although he has spoken plainly enough. She has perhaps latched onto the word 'pose' (51) and assumed that the whole of Angelo's speech is only a theoretical discussion. Her reply, 'I had rather give my body than my soul' (56) is not wholly clear.

Angelo's reply makes his intentions even more clear; he tells her that 'compell'd sins' (57) are not serious. She need not fear for her soul if she gives in to him. At last Isabella seems to understand his drift, and expresses alarm: 'How say you?' (58). To make sense of Angelo's reaction we have to infer that Isabella's voice carries either horror, disgust, incredulity or some such emotion strong enough to convince Angelo that, for the moment, a tactical retreat must be made. So he pretends that the discussion they are having is purely theoretical. However, he has gone too far to turn back and, steeling himself for a second onslaught, puts the proposition again. The sense of having suffered a reversal, but being prepared to ready himself for a fresh attempt, can effectively be rendered by a substantial pause in the middle of line 60, immediately before 'Answer to this.'

This time, he plays safe and is less direct:

> Might there not be a charity in sin
> To save this brother's life?   (63–4)

Isabella misconstrues him, deliberately or by mistake. If deliberately, to indicate obliquely, without using a crude rebuff, that his proposition is unthinkable; if by mistake, because she cannot bring herself to believe that Angelo could be so wicked. At all events, she takes him to mean that saving Claudio's life would be sinful for him, because his moral duty is to punish culprits severely. In answer to this point, she offers to take the guilt upon herself – something, one notes in passing, theologically preposterous. Isabella, as one about to enter the religious life, must know that such a shifting of moral responsibility is impossible before God. Perhaps it is an example of her saying something she does not mean in order to gain an advantage. Later in the scene, she pleads guilty to this very thing:

> O pardon me, my lord; it oft falls out
> To have what we would have, we speak not what we mean.   (117–18)

And we have already seen a further possible example at line 50.

For seven more lines (67–73) the two continue to speak at cross-purposes. Angelo refers to the sin and he means fornication, whereas for Isabella the sin is leniency. Angelo becomes impatient and resolves to 'speak more gross' (82); that is to say, more plainly. But he does not do so. He continues to pretend that they are talking of some imagined 'person' (91), someone 'suppos'd' (97), and puts his question for the third time. Isabella's answer now is unhesitating:

>     . . . were I under the terms of death,
>     Th'impression of keen whips I'd wear as rubies,
>     And strip myself to death as to a bed
>     That longing have been sick for, ere I'd yield
>     My body up to shame.   (100–4)

The vehemence is unmistakable. And the violence of the language ('strip' and 'whip') together with the evocation of blood ('rubies') has a sexual, more specifically a masochistic, force. The speech also anticipates one by Claudio on the same theme (III.i.82–4) which is altogether more serene.

It is often said that Isabella should have acquiesced in Angelo's demand. What, modern readers ask, is the loss of chastity compared to the death of a brother? Some critics have made this a serious problem and, searching for reasons, have suggested that, for example, Isabella is a hysteric so frightened of sexuality, so revolted, that not even the threat of death can prevail with her. But the real answer may lie in the next speech:

>     Better it were a brother died at once,
>     Than that a sister, by redeeming him,
>     Should die for ever.   (106–8)

There we have it: the fear of eternal damnation. Compared with that the death of a man is a mere nothing. It is also worth pointing out that one of the commonplaces of the literature of the period is that death is a friend. We find a classic statement of it in the Duke's speech to Claudio, 'Be absolute for death' (III.i.5–41). Such an attitude provides a second clue perhaps to Isabella's being prepared to let her brother die.

The discussion about human frailty (121–37) is another clever example of the cross-purposes dialogue. Isabella is talking about the frailty involved in her brother's offence, and then later in the general sense of susceptibility to sin. Angelo, however, at 12 ('We are all frail') and 123 ('Nay, women are frail too') is trying to place in Isabella's mind the idea of an understandable sexual wantonness in women, so as to make her hoped-for surrender seem more excusable, even natural, to her.

Isabella's speech on women's frailty concludes with the following view:

> For we are soft as our complexions are,
> And credulous to false prints.   (128-9)

The word 'credulous' means 'easily accepting', and Angelo takes Isabella's words to amount practically to an admission that she is now prepared to give in. This is why he makes his demand yet again, albeit rather obliquely, telling her to put on 'the destin'd livery' (137).

Finally, Angelo does make her understand his intentions:

> Believe me, on mine honour,
> My words express my purpose.   (146-7)

The second line's directness reminds us that so much spoken up to this point has been devious and muddled.

In Isabella's reply, the word 'honour' - which we have already seen her use with unwitting irony at 34, and II.ii.158 and 162 - is thrown back in his face. Isabella's reply is not merely a defiant rejection of Angelo's proposal; she retorts with a forceful threat of her own:

> Sign me a present pardon for my brother,
> Or with an outstretch'd throat I'll tell the world aloud
> What man thou art.   (151-3)

Now that matters are out in the open, Angelo's frustration finds vent in a malicious refinement of his threat. Claudio will not only be executed but also tortured slowly. The alliterative 'die the death' (164) and 'death draw out' (165) give a cruel emphasis to his words.

Isabella's closing soliloquy expresses a confidence about her brother's expected resolve in the face of death which, of course, is misplaced. Once again, we note the violence of the language (and, yet again, the ironic use of 'honour'):

> Yet hath he in him such a mind of honour,
> That had he twenty heads to tender down
> On twenty bloody blocks, he'd yield them up
> Before his sister should her body stoop
> To such abhorr'd pollution.   (178-82)

The vehemence of her words anticipates the near-hysteria of her reaction when Claudio fails to live up to her expectations and begs his sister to give in to Angelo and thus spare his life, at III.i.135–46 ('O. you beast . . .').

## Act III, Scene i

### Summary
The disguised Duke visits Claudio in prison and argues that he should welcome death, because life is painful and miserable. Claudio reconciles himself to death temporarily. However, when Isabella visits him, he looks to her for some hope of life. She reveals to him Angelo's proposal. At first, Claudio says that he is prepared to die rather than that his sister should give in to Angelo, but as they talk he becomes weaker in resolve and finally pleads with her to save his life. Isabella is furious and denounces his weakness mercilessly. The Duke intervenes, telling Claudio that Angelo's ultimatum to Isabella was made merely to test her. He must prepare to die.

Claudio exits and Vincentio then tells Isabella that he has a plan by which she can save her brother's life and also fulfil Angelo's demand. He tells her of Mariana, who was betrothed to Angelo until the latter broke off the engagement because Mariana's dowry had been lost at sea. If Mariana were to visit Angelo in place of Isabella, so that their relationship would be sexually consummated, Angelo would be placed in a position of feeling bound in honour to wed Mariana. Isabella agrees to this 'bed-trick'.

### Commentary
The sentiments expressed by the Duke in his speech, 'Be absolute for death' (5–41) stem partly from the attitudes of a group of ancient Roman philosophers, the Stoics, and partly from Christianity. Although Vincentio argues that life is contemptible and full of misery, there is no mention of the consolation for this state of affairs, namely, the possibility of eternal bliss in the after-life. One would expect a friar (even a pretended one) to include this, especially as one assumes that the Duke's purpose in speaking is to offer comfort to Claudio.

Some of the arguments advanced in the speech are similar to those found in much seventeenth-century poetry, in particular, in the work of a group of poets called the *Metaphysicals*. Very often we find Metaphysical poets employing comparisons and arguments which, although intellectually ingenious and witty, have little logic. This is the case here. For example, the view that we are not noble because our worldly comforts have lowly origins (they may be 'traced back to the shambles and the dunghill' according to Dr Johnson's interpretation of these lines [13–15]) hardly makes sense, because people rarely feel that they are base for this reason. Again, the notion that people are cowardly for fearing worms (15–17) is defective. It is surely the process of dying, and the fear of damnation, which people have uppermost in their minds, rather than the physical condition of their corpses.

Next, we have the comparison of death to sleep. The argument is that sleep is desirable, and yet we fear death which is nothing more than a sleep (17-19). The logical error here is that we enjoy not sleep itself so much as entering it with a pleasant anticipation of *temporary* oblivion followed by the pleasure of waking from it refreshed. People on their deathbeds have none of these pleasures. There is, too, the more obvious point that the mind is active during sleep but defunct in death.

I stress the illogic of these points because what is being shown to us is that people may be comforted and given genuine reassurance with flimsy arguments, just as they can be won over in a debate by the same means. Frequently, it is the kindness of the consoler, not the words spoken, which soothe. And the Duke's words appear to have had this soothing effect, for Claudio's reaction is to resign himself to the inevitable:

> I humbly thank you.
> To sue to live, I find I seek to die,
> And seeking death, find life. Let it come on.   (41-3)

The fine 'literary' combination here of antithesis and paradox (again, typically Metaphysical) brings to a close this opening part of the scene whose style is essentially that of formal and elaborate speech. On Isabella's entrance, we return to quick-fire dramatic exchanges.

There is an irony in Claudio's first question to Isabella: 'Now, sister, what's the comfort?' (53). It is not just that she brings the very opposite of comfort. It also shows that, although a person might express a sincere resolution to welcome death ('I find I seek to die' [42]) only a minute later that same person has reverted to the original fear. Claudio is now saying that once again he has a 'hope to live' (4). Human beings cling tenaciously to life, however impoverished it is.

Isabella's delay, under persistent questioning, in telling Claudio how he might be saved, is clearly based on her fear that he will want her to save his life by agreeing to Angelo's proposal: 'O, I do fear thee, Claudio' (73). She is, of course, right in this fear, as events show, but this attitude towards her brother is inconsistent with her earlier view (II.iv.179-82).

In the previous scene, we noted how Isabella's preparedness to die was couched in violent language: 'keen whips', 'strip myself to death' (II.iv.101, 102). Here, Claudio's (albeit temporary) acceptance of death is, by contrast, expressed in an image of moving serenity:

> If I must die,
> I will encounter darkness as a bride
> And hug it in mine arms.   (82-4)

Again, we see Shakespeare's love of contrasts. The coldness of death is articulated in an image of great warmth and intimacy.

When Isabella does finally reveal Angelo's proposal, she conveys the information in a rhetorical question, thereby considerably strengthening his sense of her wanting him to be outraged:

> Dost thou think, Claudio,
> If I would yield him my virginity
> Thou mightst be free?    (96-8)

The remainder of the dialogue between brother and sister represents a fine account of the complex fluctuations and interraction between two people. Claudio's 'Thou shalt not do't' (102) sounds determined, but its very emphasis indicates wavering. When Isabella replies that, if it were her life rather than her chastity that was threatened, she would gladly give it up, Claudio says: 'Thanks, dear Isabel' (105). This line combines despondency with a weak sense of 'being brave'. Isabella does not help by inadvertently harping on the imminence of Claudio's death, through her use of 'tomorrow' (102, 106). (There are fully fourteen references in the play to Claudio's dying 'tomorrow' and three further references to the haste of his execution.)

The process of Claudio's weakening continues. He argues that if a wise man like Angelo is prepared to sin, perhaps the sin is not so serious. This thought develops into a full and poetically heightened disquisition on death which offsets the Duke's earlier speech (5-41). Claudio dwells on the torments awaiting the spirit after death, torments based not on Christian teaching but on the writings of classical authors. For example, his fear of the 'thrilling region of thick-ribbed ice' (122) is a reference to the 'cold' purgatory described by Virgil in his *Aeneid*, Book 6, and deemed appropriate as a punishment for sins of passion. Just as it is an oddity that the Duke should have omitted any reference to the promise of heaven in his speech at the beginning of the scene, so here it is odd that Claudio should assume that on his death he will be damned. He appears to have no expectation of salvation, even though his predicament – one in which he knows the time of his own death – is especially advantageous, according to the tenets of theology, because it means that he can prepare himself for death through repentence and place himself in a state of grace. (These advantages are referred to explicitly when the substitute execution of Barnardine is being discussed in IV.iii.)

Isabella's reaction to Claudio's fears – 'Alas, alas' (131) – is not a sympathetic echo of agreement with her brother's speech, but a registering of her fear that his argument is a sign of weakness leading, as indeed it does, to his plea: 'Sweet sister, let me live' (132).

When he does make that plea, Isabella's wrath is disproportionate and hysterical. It leads her to yet another far-fetched analogy:

> Is't not a kind of incest, to take life
> From thine own sister's shame?   (138-9)

and to astonishing callousness:

> Might but my bending down
> Reprieve thee from thy fate, it should proceed.   (143-4)

In her refusal to understand, or make the slightest allowances, for someone in the grip of fear, she demonstrates the same hard inflexibility for which she has rightly denounced Angelo.

The Duke now intervenes and assures Claudio that death is to be his fate. Claudio, a great vacillator, once again has a change of heart: 'I am so out of love with life that I will sue to be rid of it' (170-1).

Isabella's dialogue with Vincentio, which concludes the scene, contains three interesting features. First, in expressing her determination to deny Angelo, she tells the Duke: 'I had rather my brother die by the law, than my son should be unlawfully born' (188-90). This is a considerable change from the previous formula: 'More than our brother is our chastity'(II.iv.184). Secondly, on hearing Mariana's sad history, she remarks: 'What a merit were it in death to take this poor maid from the world!' (231-2). This welcoming of death is of course a contrast to Claudio's fear of it, but it also repeats a commonplace of the period, that death was not to be grudgingly accepted, but welcomed as a friend and comforter.

Thirdly, Isabella's swift acceptance of the 'bed-trick' has often been thought to be at odds with her moral stance over Claudio's offence. Critics have offered various excuses for her apparent double standard: that Angelo and Mariana are not in quite the same position as Claudio and Juliet, and that she agrees because the trick is proposed by someone she takes to be a friar and therefore one who would never suggest anything improper. Nevertheless, I think we are entitled to feel at least some unease at Isabella's acquiescence.

## Act III, Scene ii

*Summary*
Constable Elbow has arrested Pompey for brothel-keeping, and is in the process of bringing him in when they are met by the Duke, who denounces Pompey's trade. Lucio enters and not only refuses to stand bail for his friend Pompey, but laughs at his predicament. When he is left alone with the Duke, he pretends to be an intimate of Vincentio's and, not of course realising the identity of his interlocutor, slanders him. Vincentio is very angry and tells him that he will have to answer for his words later. Lucio exits.

Overdone enters, also being taken to prison. We learn from her that
Lucio has a child by a prostitute called Mistress Kate Keep-down. Vincentio
asks Escalus about the character of the supposedly absent Duke, and
receives flattering replies. In a final soliloquy, Vincentio condemns Angelo's
hypocrisy and says that he will have to use scheming to counteract Angelo's
evil.

## Commentary

The Duke's attitude to sexual misconduct is severe, and certainly closer to
the punitive views of Angelo than to the attitudes of Escalus or the Provost.
We see this in Vincentio's sharp condemnation of Pompey ('Fie, sirrah . . .!
[18-26]) and in his reply to Lucio, who is complaining of the new deputy's
strictness: 'It is too general a vice, and severity must cure it' (96). It is
underlined by his use of the phrase 'filthy vice' (22) which is exactly
Angelo's phrase at II.iv.42.

Lucio's behaviour throughout the scene represents him at his worst.
The arrested Pompey welcomes his approach with, 'Here's a gentleman,
and a friend of mine' (40-1), but Lucio is soon to prove neither. Not
content with refusing to stand bail, this fair-weather friend actually mocks
Pompey and gloats over his discomfiture. Later, when regaling the disguised
Vincentio with his tissue of scandalous lies, he is guilty of an offence –
false report – which was considered far more serious in an age when so
much information was passed by word of mouth. James I was especially
severe with the spreaders of false rumours, and the Duke reverts to the
theme at 179-83 ('No might nor greatness . . .) and at IV.i.60-5 ('O place
and greatness . . .'). Lucio's breaking of his promise to marry Kate Keep-
down parallels Angelo's treatment of Mariana. At the end of the play,
both men are forced to marry the women they have wronged.

Vincentio's angry denial of Lucio's slanders indicates a rather unattractive self-esteem:

Let him be but testimonied in his own bringings-forth, and he shall
appear to the envious a scholar, a statesman, and a soldier.   (140-2)

This serves to remind us once again that although the nature of Vincentio's
role might predispose us to think of him as the very embodiment of virtue
and justice, he does have character flaws of his own, much like Prospero in
The Tempest, with whom he is frequently compared.

Obviously upset by Lucio's remarks, the Duke later turns to Escalus to
massage his wounded pride, asking 'of what disposition was the duke?'
(224-5) The reply is flattering: 'One that, above all other strifes, contended
especially to know himself' (226-7). Whilst we are prepared to accept the
truth of this, we do wonder a little at such a blatant exercise in fishing for
compliments.

In addition to the comic richness of an exchange in which Lucio unwittingly slanders the Duke to his face, the episode creates suspense by giving promise of a further scene – one of reckoning – in which Lucio will have to answer for his words. This duly takes place in V.i.

## Act IV, Scene i

### Summary
The Duke visits Mariana and introduces her to Isabella. Isabella explains the 'bed-trick' to Mariana, who is prepared to take part. Vincentio gives an assurance that the trick is not sinful.

### Commentary
It is appropriate that our first view of Mariana should be that of a sad figure listening to a song of love forsworn; she is still hopelessly in love with the man who wronged her.

On meeting Isabella, the Duke asks: 'What is the news from this good deputy?' (27) and the bitter irony of 'good' shows the full extent of Vincentio's anger at his corrupt deputy.

The assignation is to take place not indoors, but in a garden, and some have felt this would remind audiences of the Garden of Eden, the scene of man's Fall. Certainly the details of the garden's seclusion – surrounded by a wall, hidden by a vineyard, protected by both a gate and a 'little door' (32) – emphasise the dark and disreputable purpose to which it is to be put. Additionally, we know from contemporary accounts that city suburbs in England had 'garden houses' which were used for illicit lovers' meetings. Medieval literature sometimes features a garden of love, and there is a famous example in Chaucer's *The Merchant's Tale*.

## Act IV, Scene ii

### Summary
The Provost offers Pompey his freedom if he will agree to assist the executioner Abhorson. He agrees. Claudio is summoned and shown his death warrant, to be carried out the following morning. The Duke arrives and repeatedly expresses confidence that a pardon for Claudio will soon be received. Instead, the message from Angelo is that Claudio be executed even earlier than originally decided, and that his head be sent to Angelo. The Duke persuades the Provost to spare Claudio and to agree to execute another prisoner, Barnardine, whose guilt in his crime has only recently been established, and to send Barnardine's head to Angelo instead of Claudio's.

## Commentary

In this scene, Shakespeare once again uses the apparently inconsequential comic exchanges of 'low' characters to underpin the main concerns of the play. Abhorson's complaint that Pompey is unfit to assist him because he is a bawd, places him in a similar position to Angelo. Both are imperfect men who seek to pass judgement on others without examining their own offences. The Provost spells out the point in rebuking Abhorson: 'Go to, sir, you weigh equally: a feather will turn the scale' (28–9).

Once the Duke has arrived at the prison, the Provost yet again complains at Angelo's severity towards Claudio. Vincentio's reply is especially interesting:

> Not so, not so; his life is parallel'd
> Even with the stroke and line of his great justice.
> He doth with holy abstinence subdue
> That in himself which he spurs on his power
> To qualify in others: were he meal'd with that
> Which he corrects, then were he tyrannous;
> But this being so, he's just.   (77–83)

It is, of course, pure irony; Vincentio knows full well that Angelo, far from having 'subdued' himself, is guiltier than the man he has condemned. (This technique is called 'dramatic irony' and refers to occasions when the audience and/or some characters in the play have an 'inside' knowledge of understanding of some circumstances not available to other characters.)

Before the arrival of Angelo's messenger, the Duke states his expectation of a pardon four times within sixteen lines. This has the effect of making Angelo's reneging on his promise all the more shocking when revealed in the message.

In describing Barnardine's mental state, the Provost talks of a man 'that apprehends death no more dreadfully but as a drunken sleep' (140–1). We are immediately reminded of the Duke's comparison of sleep and death in III.i:

> Thy best of rest is sleep;
> And that thou oft provok'st, yet grossly fear'st
> Thy death, which is no more.   (III.i.17–19)

The contexts of the two speeches are quite different. The point to seize upon is that here we have a fine example of Shakespeare echoing his own imagery.

## Act IV, Scene iii

*Summary*

In the prison, Pompey and Abhorson rouse Barnardine from his sleep and tell him that he is to be executed. He refuses to submit, because he has been drinking and is in no fit state to die. The Duke enters and has to agree that it would be damnable to take Barnardine's life at the present moment. The Provost arrives with the news that a pirate called Ragozine has just died in the prison; he suggests that this man's head be used instead of Barnardine's. The Duke agrees and orders that Claudio and Barnardine be held in a secret part of the prison, so that the Provost will not get into trouble from Angelo for failing to execute them.

Isabella arrives, and the Duke pretends to her that Claudio is already dead. Isabella is very angry and Vincentio promises that she will have revenge if she trusts in him. Lucio enters, sad at the supposed death of Claudio. Once again he criticises the Duke to the disguised Vincentio.

*Commentary*

The attempt by Pompey and Abhorson to bring Barnardine to some awareness of his predicament is a comic contrast to the scene in which another prisoner, Claudio, has to face his death (III.i). For example, the sombre comparison of death to sleep in the earlier scene, becomes here a jibe:

> Pray, Master Barnardine, awake till you are executed, and sleep afterwards. (31-2)

The comedy partly depends on a reversal of power. A drunken reprobate simply refuses to be executed because he is not ready. He speaks as though he were in charge of his own destiny, rather than being at the mercy of others: 'If you have anything to say to me, come to my ward: for thence will not I today' (61-2). This proud insistence on his own personal independence under threat of death contrasts with Claudio's fearful vacillations in the same circumstances.

Immediately prior to Isabella's entrance, Vincentio explains his reason for withholding the knowledge of Claudio's safety from her:

> To make her heavenly comforts of despair
> When it is least expected. (109-10)

For the most part, the Duke's behind-the-scenes manipulations have been hitherto benign. With this decision, which inevitably causes Isabella great distress, Vincentio takes his interference too far. He is playing God with the emotions of a real person, and being cruel without justification.

The wording that Vincentio uses to tell Isabella of her brother's supposed death starts as though the news it contains is happy: 'He hath releas'd him, Isabel, - from the world' (114). It is strongly reminiscent of the diction she herself used to Claudio (III.i.55-60) which has been commented upon above.

Isabella's initial reaction to the news is fury: 'O, I will to him and pluck out his eyes!' (119). Once again we see the flash of emotion that was especially apparent in her two interviews with Angelo (II.ii; II.iv). In counselling patience, Vincentio promises that she will have 'revenges' (135) on Angelo in due course. This seems to be rather at odds with Vincentio's role as a holy friar supposedly committed to Christian notions of forgiveness. Perhaps it is a preparing of the ground for his testing of Isabella's disposition to mercy in V.i.

Lucio's genuine distress at what he takes to be the death of his friend Claudio makes him partly blame Vincentio: 'if the old fantastical duke of dark corners had been at home, he had lived' (156-7). It is amusing that he should describe the Duke as 'fantastical' (he does it earlier, at III.ii.89) for he himself is described as 'a Fantastic' in the list of characters in the First Folio in 1623. Also, when he refers to the 'duke of dark corners' he is thinking of what he takes, or pretends to take, to be Vincentio's habit of making illicit sexual assignations. But in another sense, bearing in mind the secret plotting and disguise, Vincentio is indeed a 'duke of dark corners'.

## Act IV, Scene iv

### Summary
Escalus and Angelo are perplexed by the instructions they have received from Vincentio about the latter's return. They do not understand why they are told to meet him at the city gates. We discover that there is to be a proclamation, encouraging those who seek redress for injustice to come forward. Escalus departs, and in a soliloquy Angelo is seen to be in great anxiety about his crime. He believes that Isabella will not acuse him publicly because of her sexual modesty. He explains that he felt he had to order Claudio's execution because he feared that, had he been allowed to live, he would have taken revenge.

### Commentary
Escalus says of the Duke's communications: 'Every letter he hath writ hath disvouched other' (1). It is not clear why this is part of Vincentio's plan, or what effect it is supposed to have.

The detail about the proclamation gives the audience a comforting sense that justice will soon be done, in full public view, and Angelo made to account for himself.

In his soliloquy, Angelo expresses confidence in his safety. His reputation is so strong that scandal cannot touch him. This is typical of the play's dramatic irony, for the audience knows full well that the Duke has enough evidence to expose Angelo completely.

Angelo is not indifferent to his crime. Twice, he regrets Claudio's death: 'He should have liv'd' (26); 'Would yet he had liv'd' (30). His general observation that 'Nothing goes right' (32) once a person has embarked on an evil course can clearly be seen as a central theme of the play, borne out by all the entanglements and complexities stemming from Angelo's decision to threaten Isabella.

## Act IV, Scene v

*Summary*
The Duke, no longer in disguise, gives letters to Friar Peter and tells him to hold to the course which has already been determined between them off-stage. Varrius enters and Vincentio announces that other friends will soon be arriving.

*Commentary*
The purpose of the scene appears to be to remind the audience that the Duke is fully in control of the situation, that he has many helpers, and that he is taking measures to ensure that justice will finally be done. The introduction of the names of as many as four characters (Flavius, Valencius, Rowland and Crassus) never mentioned before, and not mentioned subsequently, is dramatically untidy and might mislead audiences into imagining subsequent roles for them.

## Act IV, Scene vi

*Summary*
Isabella and Mariana are discussing the instructions that the disguised Vincentio has given them. Isabella has been told to lie and she is uneasy about it; Mariana tells her to have confidence in the pretended friar. We learn that Isabella has been warned that, when she accuses Angelo publicly, Vincentio may speak against her, but that everything will be satisfactorily resolved in the end.

Friar Peter enters and announces that the Duke is about to enter the city and that he has picked out for them a place where they may stand so as to be able to have access to the Duke as he passes.

*Commentary*

This brief exchange serves to give us advance warning of the odd behaviour of the Duke in the next scene.

Isabella's preparedness to lie appears to be a further example of her having almost suspended her own moral judgement and allowed it to be taken over by Vincentio whom she believes can counsel no wrong.

## Act V, Scene i

*Summary*

Angelo and Escalus welcome the Duke back. He praises them for the quality of justice they have dispensed in his absence. Isabella comes forward and denounces Angelo to the Duke, who pretends to think her mad. From this point onwards, Lucio adds his own comments and is repeatedly silenced by Vincentio. Isabella's story is true except that she conceals the 'bed-trick' and pretends that Angelo slept with her rather than Mariana. Vincentio pretends to think her story incredible and he orders her arrest for spreading scandal. Isabella mentions Friar Lodowick to Vincentio, as one who has knowledge of the affair. (Lodowick was the name assumed by the Duke when he was disguised.) Lucio says that Lodowick spoke slanders against the Duke in his presence, and that he is an impertinent and unpleasant fellow. Friar Peter contradicts Lucio and speaks of Lodowick's good character. He says that Lodowick is ill and that he is speaking on his behalf.

Mariana enters, veiled. After much obscure hinting, and some quibbling incomprehensible to her listeners, and only making sense to the audience, she states that she took Isabella's place at the secret assignation in the garden. Angelo denies this. The Duke orders that Angelo and Escalus should hear the case; he also commands that Friar Lodowick be produced. He then exits, returning in the disguise of Lodowick. He describes Angelo as a villain and blames the Duke for leaving the case to be heard by the accused man. Escalus is angry at his impudence and orders him to be taken to prison. There is a struggle which ends when Lucio plucks off the friar's hood, thus revealing Lodowick's true identity.

Angelo, realising he is exposed, admits his guilt and asks for the death sentence. Vincentio orders that he wed Mariana immediately; Angelo and Mariana exit for this purpose. The Duke continues to pretend to Isabella that Claudio is dead, making an excuse for his failure to intercede in time.

When Angelo returns with his new bride, Vincentio sentences him to death. All Mariana's pleas for mercy for her husband are rejected. She turns to Isabella and begs help from her in pleading with the Duke. Isabella kneels down and asks Vincentio to be merciful towards Angelo. He again refuses. He then dismisses the Provost from his office for having Claudio executed at an unusual hour, and orders Barnardine to be brought to him. Barnardine is brought in, together with Claudio blindfolded. The Duke pardons Barnardine. The Provost removes Claudio's blindfold and Vincentio tells Isabella that her brother is pardoned. Because Claudio is still alive, Angelo is saved from execution. Vincentio then asks Isabella to marry him. Vincentio now turns to Lucio and orders that he must marry the woman he has wronged and afterwards he must be whipped and hanged. Vincentio immediately relents, cancelling the penalties of whipping and hanging, but insisting on the marriage.

In his concluding speech, Vincentio speaks to Angelo of Mariana's virtue; he thanks Escalus for his goodness and promises to promote the Provost, and he repeats his proposal of marriage to Isabella.

*Commentary*

Shakespeare packs his concluding scene with one example after another of dramatic irony; that is to say, speeches are made, especially by the Duke, which have a significance for the audience quite at odds with the surface meaning. In greeting Angelo and Escalus, Vincentio says that he has 'made enquiry of you' (5) and this of course is taken by them to mean that others have sent him good reports whilst he was away; but he is in fact referring to his own behind-the-scenes probing.

Repeatedly, Vincentio applauds Angelo's supposed virtues: at 107–15 ('by heaven . . .'); at 241–4 ('think'st thou thy oaths . . .') and in a host of brief remarks. The dramatic excitement of such speeches lies in the audience's awareness not merely that the opposite is the truth but that we know Vincentio is creating in Angelo a false sense of security. This building-up of the strength of position of a character only to dash him more completely to the ground is typically Shakespearean.

Vincentio's aim is not merely to bring Angelo to justice, but to make him display publicly the evil which has contaminated him. The Duke pretends to support Angelo's reputation for virtue in the scene, when actually he is giving the deputy rope to hang himself. Angelo's denunciation of Isabella as a madwoman ('her wits I fear me are not firm' [35]), his repetition of the slander against Mariana, that she was guilty of moral laxness, and finally his request to Vincentio that he be allowed to judge and punish both women – a perversion of justice echoing his earlier abuse of judicial office – all blacken his character even further. Thus, Vincentio delays Angelo's exposure in order to force his deputy to make a public parade of that evil which hitherto he has only practised secretly. And not only that. Vincentio's bogus praise might have been expected to shame Angelo into confessing his offences, and the slight possibility that this might indeed take place – especially in view of Angelo's previous twinges of conscience (II.ii.162-87; IV.iv.17-32) – is always in the back of the audience's mind as a possible route for the plot to take.

Angelo's eventual admission of guilt, made only when it cannot possibly be avoided, contains no element of remorse for the suffering he has caused. We have to wait a hundred lines before any penitence is expressed:

> I am sorry that such sorrow I procure,
> And so deep sticks it in my penitent heart
> That I crave death more willingly than mercy;
> 'Tis my deserving, and I do entreat it.   (472-5)

The question of whether these sentiments are genuine has been a matter of controversy. The fact that the words are spoken by a man already sentenced to death, and therefore with nothing to gain from expressing them, would seem to suggest that Angelo is being sincere. We also recall the twinges of conscience that he registered earlier. Nevertheless, there is something suspect in the suddenness of the repentance. But there are other examples of such sudden repentance in Shakespeare – most notable, the villain Edmund's repentance at the end of *King Lear* – and it could be argued that we are asked to accept the swiftness of the change of heart as a literary convention, much like the improbabilities of the play. At this point, Shakespeare is more interested in establishing the general point that evildoers can be brought to a proper sense of their guilt, than he is in portraying a psychologically convincing example of it.

Angelo is not the only person whom Vincentio manipulates. He also subjects Isabella to a double test. First, she has to have the courage to come forward as Angelo's public accuser, without the supportive presence of the friar who prompted her to it; and she has to lie about the 'bed-trick', despite her own reservations about such deceit. This is essentially a test of her trust. Will she be able to place herself publicly in what seems like an untenable and indeed dangerous position because she has faith in Lodowick? She passes this test.

The second and more important test is to establish whether she has learnt the moral of all the foregoing events: that justice must be tempered with mercy. Vincentio has engineered matters so that Isabella is called upon to plead for Angelo at a time when she still believes her own brother dead. For her, therefore, it is no mere abstraction but an issue in which her whole emotional being is engaged. The Duke makes her hard choice even harder by pretending to feel that a spirit of vengeance in Isabella would be reasonable and just:

> Should she kneel down in mercy of this fact,
> Her brother's ghost his paved bed would break,
> And take her hence in horror.   (432-4)

Isabella has learnt the lesson of mercy. It is a skilful advocate who can think of arguments in favour of a man like Angelo, and as she speaks we are reminded of her brother's words earlier:

> she hath prosperous art
> When she will play with reason and discourse,
> And well she can persuade.   (I.ii.174-6)

The actual arguments she employs in her plea for mercy (441-52) are of two kinds. In the first half of the speech, there is an attempt to excuse Angelo by a series of points whose illogic reminds us of similar arguments in II.ii. She asks Vincentio to look on Angelo 'As if my brother liv'd' (443). This is equivalent to a lawyer at a murder trial expecting the judge to pretend that the dead victim was unhurt. (It is, of course, complicated by the dramatic irony in the situation: Claudio is indeed alive.) She then goes on:

> I partly think
> A due sincerity govern'd his deeds
> Till he did look on me.   (443-5)

It could surely be said of all criminals, however odious, that perhaps they acted properly until they were tempted not to, that they were reasonably good until the first occasion when they were bad. It is not an impressive defence. The point is that Isabella's preparedness to plead for Angelo is such that she is willing to dredge up anything which might help in the difficult task of presenting a defence.

The second part of the defence is much sounder, and purely legalistic. Human courts of justice can only condemn if crimes are actually perpetrated; a mere intention to do wrong is something which, by implication here, only God can punish. This distinction between human and divine justice has been made by Isabella before. When Angelo had equated murder and fornication, she had pointed out that although they were equally grave in the eyes of God, they were not so viewed in human courts: 'Tis set down so in heaven, but not in earth' (II.iv.50). Because all humans are fallible, and judges have faults just like the people they punish, human justice needs to be more circumspect than the justice of heaven: this is the gist of her argument. Isabella goes far beyond the call of duty in speaking on Angelo's behalf. Whereas the Duke's mercy towards the various offenders might be said to stem from concepts of wise governance, her merciful impulse surely arises from generosity, forgiveness and a sympathy with Mariana. Nevertheless, her plea lacks the warmth of her earlier appeal for her brother in II.ii. Both the phrasing and the diction suggest the coldly analytical.

Immediately after Isabella's discovery that her brother is alive, Vincentio proposes marriage to her. He links the proposal to Claudio's pardon in such a way as to suggest that Isabella should be grateful to him for favouring her brother and should show that gratitude by accepting his proposal:

> If he be like your brother, for his sake
> Is he pardon'd; and for your lovely sake
> Give me your hand and say you will be mine. (488-90)

If 'moral blackmail' is perhaps too strong a term for this, we can certainly describe it as undue pressure. The Duke uses Claudio's life as a pawn in his game of seduction just as Angelo had done. Clearly, the two cases are not equal in terms of culpability but they are of the same nature.

Isabella does not respond to the proposal; nor do we hear from her when it is indirectly repeated at 531-4 ('Dear Isabel . . .'). There are two schools of thought on this silence. The first argues that Shakespearean comedies always end in the marriage of the major characters; audiences of the period would have taken Isabella's acceptance so much for granted that any verbal sign of such agreement would not have been strictly necessary. Or, to put the argument another way, it would have been unthinkable for a Shakespearean comedy to end with the 'heroine' refusing to marry the 'hero'. One of the defining characteristics of comedy is, after all, the reconciliation and concord of the dénouement, and marriage is the most potent symbol of that concord.

Nevertheless, the silence is unusual and directors of the play have occasionally taken advantage of it to introduce some stage business, such as Isabella turning away or assuming a countenance of displeasure or even shock, indicating either her refusal, or at least lack of enthusiasm.

It is sometimes suggested that the mercy Vincentio shows in this scene – he forgives Barnardine, Claudio, and Angelo - is at odds with his repeated insistence on the need for enforcing Vienna's 'strict statutes and most biting laws' (I.iii.19). The answer often given is that, along with the other characters, the Duke has learnt the valuable lesson of the play: not to judge harshly.

Some have singled out Vincentio's treatment of Lucio as unreasonably severe: he is forced to marry a 'punk' (520). But we can surely see this as equivalent to Angelo's situation in regard to Mariana. Both men have wronged a woman whom they promised to marry and both are forced to honour their promises.

# 4 THEMES AND ISSUES

## 4.1 JUSTICE AND MERCY

The question of whether this play is recommending severity or mercy in dealing with offences against the law is uncertain. A chief reason for this is that the arguments advanced for both are strong, and individual characters are found to be supporting severity at one moment, but mercy at another.

The Duke is a good example of this apparent fickleness. His main reason for handing over temporary power to Angelo is to ensure that the law which he himself has neglected is enforced. The language which he uses to explain this to Friar Thomas (I.iii) is the language of severity. The 'strict statutes and most biting laws' (19) must be enforced; fathers who merely display the 'threatening twigs of birch' (24) without using them to beat their children are seriously misguided; his desire is to 'strike and gall' (36) offenders. In a later scene (III.ii) his abusive speech to Pompey is in similar terms: Pompey is 'wicked' (18) and is guilty of 'filthy vice' (22); he is 'stinkingly depending' (26) on the, abominable and beastly touches' (23) of his brothel customers. Vincentio turns to the constable and says:

> Take him to prison, officer:
> Correction and instruction must both work
> Ere this rude beast will profit.   (30-2)

And yet, despite this firmness throughout the play, in the final scene he is the chief instrument of extreme mercy: Angelo and Lucio are forced to marry the women they wronged, but apart from that the four offenders (Barnardine and Claudio are the other two) go unpunished. It is clear, too, that he expects and hopes that Isabella will show mercy towards Angelo.

The same contradictions exist in the character of Escalus. He is a judge and accepts the need for severity, but is himself remarkably lenient to Froth and Pompey in the trial scene (II.i). Indeed, his leniency is probably

46

the reason why he is passed over for deputy by Vincentio, who wants to be certain that he appoints someone strict.

The position is further confused because of the nature of the arguments used by Escalus to persuade Angelo to be lenient with Claudio. First, he urges the fact that Claudio 'had a most noble father' (II.i.7). Even granted the greater importance attached to parentage in Shakespeare's day, this is not an impressive defence. Secondly, he asks his brother deputy whether he, Angelo, might not at some time in the past have been in danger of falling into the same sin as Claudio. This second point is as feeble as the first and is swiftly dismissed by Angelo:

> 'Tis one thing to be tempted, Escalus,
> Another thing to fall.
>
> • • • • • • •
>
> When I that censure him do so offend,
> Let mine own judgement pattern out my death,
> And nothing come in partial.   (II.i.17–18; 29–31)

Like the Duke and Escalus, Isabella also seems to be uncertain as to whether severity or mercy should be employed to deal with offenders. At the beginning of her first interview with Angelo, she states:

> There is a vice that most I do abhor,
> And most desire should meet the blow of justice;
> For which I would not plead, but that I must;   (II.ii.29–31)

It is reasonable to take this to mean that, in ordinary circumstances, she would wish to see someone in Claudio's position firmly punished; but that, because of blood kinship and the ties of affection, she is obliged to argue for mercy in his particular case. Thus, all her subsequent pleas for mercy are not wholly sincere; she is simply doing her best for a close relative. The eloquence of her pleading loses some of its power when we know this. As she admits in a crucial passage:

> O pardon me, my lord; it oft falls out
> To have what we would have, we speak not what we mean.
> I something do excuse the thing I hate
> For his advantage that I dearly love.   (II.iv.117–20)

Further, when Isabella is told that Claudio has been executed, mercy and forgiveness are far from her thoughts: 'O, I will to him and pluck out his eyes!' (IV.iii.119). In the prison scene (III.i) when Claudio pleads with her to 'let me live' (132) her hysterically angry reply is completely merciless:

> Die, perish! Might but my bending down
> Reprieve thee from thy fate, it should proceed.

> I'll pray a thousand prayers for thy death;
> No word to save thee.   (143-6)

Leaving aside the question of whether she should have refused her brother's request, her denunciation of Claudio is heartless. Despite all this, in the play's final scene, Isabella displays great mercy by pleading for Angelo's life.

Where it is employed, mercy is not always either effective or appropriate. Even Escalus's patience is exhausted by the repeated offences of Mistress Overdone; being let off with warnings has had no effect:

> MISTRESS O.  Good my lord, be good to me. Your honour is accounted
>     a merciful man. Good my lord.
> ESCALUS  Double and treble admonition, and still forfeit in the same
>     kind! This would make mercy swear and play the tyrant.   (III.ii.
>     185-9)

The arguments advanced in the play in favour of mercy, as opposed to strict justice, are not intellectually impressive. For example, Isabella, in II.ii, argues that Angelo should condemn the offence but not the offender ('I do beseech you ...' [35-6]); she claims that if Angelo and Claudio were in each other's places, Claudio would not be as severe a judge towards Angelo ('If he had been ...' [64-6]); she tells Angelo that his sternness is as if God should punish him for his own sins according to his strict deserts ('How would you be ...' [75-9]); she insults him for being 'tyrannous' (109) and a 'petty officer' (113); she expects him to relent simply because he too might have a natural guiltiness ('Go to your bosom ...' [137-42]).

However, although these arguments are not intellectually convincing, they do have a strong emotional appeal. This is brought out most dramatically in Isabella's simple reply to one of Angelo's long-winded and cogent speeches rejecting the merciful approach: 'Yet show some pity' (100). The play is making it clear that human feelings must play a role, as well as logic, in human decision-making. Our hearts can be merciful even when our minds condemn, and out of that situation comes the softening of strict justice which we see in action in the final scene.

There is, of course, a further reason for tempering justice with mercy, which is concerned with neither reason nor emotion. The entire play, as signalled in the title, is based on ethical concepts to be found in the Sermon on the Mount (St Matthew, 5-7). In the sermon, Christ exhorts his listeners to reject the Old Testament doctrine of strict justice, 'an eye for an eye' (5:38-9) and urges them to forgive offenders (6:14-15). Of special importance for this play is his comment on judging others:

> Judge not, that ye be not judged. For with what judgment ye judge, ye
> shall be judged: and with what measure ye mete, it shall be measured to

you again. And why beholdest thou the mote that is in thy brother's eye, but considereth not the beam that is in thine own eye.   (7, 1–3)

Angelo is precisely in the situation of judging Claudio for a mote, whilst he has a beam of his own. And the third verse is echoed in the play's title, which seems to suggest that in strict justice, Angelo should receive the same severity which he shows to Claudio.

However, there is one serious difficulty with this biblical reading. Christ is referring in his sermon to the need for private individuals to forgive private wrongs, and not to judge them. The situation of the public official charged with the responsibility of dealing with crimes (that is, public wrongs) has always been treated quite differently by theologians. It is not for a judge to 'forgive'; if that were to happen, no judicial system could survive. Judges do not act on their own behalf and they have an obligation to enforce laws which, if not enforced, will be openly flouted, to the detriment of the whole community. Angelo, the cleverest character of the play, sees this difference between private and public function very clearly. He tells Isabella: 'It is the law, not I, condemn your brother' (II.ii.80).

For Shakespeare's contemporaries, this distinction was crucial. Princes and their appointed judges were seen as deputies of God himself; they had God's powers to punish and the injunction against judging did not apply to them. As Bishop Bilson said in his sermon at the coronation of James I in 1603, princes are 'gods by office, ruling, judging and punishing in God's stead'.

In *Measure for Measure*, there is of course the irony that strict justice can constitute a sort of mercy:

ISABELLA                         Yet show some pity.
ANGELO   I show it most of all when I show justice;
For then I pity those I do not know,
Which a dismiss'd offence would after gall,
And do him right that, answering one foul wrong,
Lives not to act another.   (II.ii.100–5)


## 4.2  SEEMING

At the beginning of the play, whilst explaining to Friar Thomas why he wishes to observe his deputy secretly, the Duke remarks:

Hence shall we see
If power change purpose, what our seemers be.   (I.iii.53–4)

Time and again we find in the play references to seeming and pretence. To Isabella, Angelo becomes an 'outward-sainted deputy' (III.i.88); to the

Duke, he is the 'well-seeming Angelo' (223). Angelo recognises the deceit in his character for himself:

> O place, O form,
> How often dost thou with thy case, thy habit,
> Wrench awe from fools, and tie the wiser souls
> To thy false seeming!   (II.iv.12-15)

A central aim of the play is to expose Angelo's hypocrisy. Many of the ironies which Shakespeare gives to the Duke in the final scene are primarily directed towards this end. For example, as the Duke greets Angelo at the start of the scene, he says:

> Give me your hand,
> And let the subject see, to make them know
> That outward courtesies would fain proclaim
> Favours that keep within.   (V.i.14-17)

The Duke is deliberately drawing attention to the fact that in Angelo's life there has not been such an agreement between what is 'outward' and what is 'within'. Much earlier, when Isabella is finally given to understand, without ambiguity, that Angelo is threatening her, her response is:

> Ha? Little honour, to be much believ'd,
> And most pernicious purpose! Seeming, seeming!
> I will proclaim thee, Angelo, look for't.   (II.iv.148-50)

It is slightly odd that she should place such an emphasis on the rather abstract idea of seeming, when one might expect her to be more exercised about Angelo's lust and cruelty. Perhaps, as Wilson Knight remarked of the play generally, it is the case here that 'we must first have regard to the central theme, and only second look for exact verisimilitude to ordinary processes of behaviour'. In other words, Shakespeare put his interest in the seeming theme before considerations of credible characterisation.

Although Angelo is at the centre of the play's concern with seeming, this is neatly counterpointed by the words and actions of the Duke. Although his motives are not so obviously disreputable, it is clear that Vincentio dissembles just as much as Angelo. As he himself admits, 'Craft against vice I must apply' (III.ii.270). He takes on a disguise, is constantly telling lies to further the aims of his intervention, and is responsible both for the 'bed-trick' and the 'head-trick' (the substitution of Ragozine's head for Claudio's). This linking of Vincentio to seeming comes to a head in the dénouement, when Lucio - and how ironic that it should be he, the Duke's adversary as it were, who is given the lines - describes Friar Lodowick as 'honest in nothing but his clothes' (V.i.261–2). The clothes are, of course, a disguise.

These images of disguise, hypocrisy and seeming are designed not merely to illustrate characteristic human duplicity. They also serve to show that the truth of any situation is not always obvious or clear to see.

# 5 TECHNICAL FEATURES

## 5.1  LANGUAGE

What language conveys is not restricted to the meaning of the individual words. Structure, phrasing, order of words, juxtaposition, rhythm, metre, tone and punctuation all modify the meaning of language. This section will draw attention to some of Shakespeare's characteristic methods of handling language and how the different techniques affect the meaning of individual speeches in this play.

Here is a straightforward example. This is the reply which Angelo gives when the Provost asks him for confirmation of Claudio's execution:

> Did I not tell thee yea? Hadst thou not order?
> Why dost thou ask again?   (II.ii.8-9)

The shortness of the three sentences, and their being clustered together, gives a clear sense of the deputy's anger. The fact that they are rhetorical questions (those where no answer is expected, as it is implied in the question itself) emphasises that anger and impatience, because it indicates his not being prepared to listen to what the Provost might have to say.

Impatience and other unsettling emotions are often conveyed in this way through the use of brevity. Angelo's 'Well: the matter?' (II.ii.33) and 'Maiden, no remedy' (48) (see also lines 19, 25, 28, 51, 53, 55, 66) make his uneasiness manifest. But brevity can be used, not merely to shed light on the character of the speaker, but also to create a particular effect on the audience. We can see this in Angelo's two speeches in II.ii (91-9, 'The law hath not been dead . . .'; 101-6, 'I show it most . . .'). They are severe, precise, correct statements of moral principles. We find ourselves intellectually satisfied, yet emotionally repelled. However cogent, there is something mean about them. Now, these two speeches are separated by Isabella's brief 'Yet show some pity' (100). There is an extraordinary power, an astonishing poignancy, in her plea, deriving much of its power precisely from its brevity. It contains a tacit admission that, at least at this stage of the argument, she is unable to counter his points. It is powerful precisely because it is feeble and pitiful, and we cannot see how she can prevail with something so insubstantial. The paucity of her words wins us over, when Angelo's intellectual rigour does not, because she speaks from the heart, and he from the head.

Metrical variation is another frequent technique. The basic Shakespearean line has ten syllables of alternating unstressed and stressed syllables: the iambic pentameter. For example:

> He doth with holy abstinence subdue   (IV.ii.79)

However the metre is regularly modified to create certain effects. For example, in the phrase, 'Merely, thou art Death's fool' (III.i.11) the last two words are both stressed. The line 'slows down' and there is a greater sense of emphasis. Exactly the same process can be seen when Isabella appeals to Angelo's inner feelings:

> Go to your bosom,
> Knock there, and ask your heart what it doth know
> That's like my brother's fault.   (II.ii.137-9)

In this example, the emphasis carried in the double stress of 'Knock there' is further increased by the comma, because the resultant pause allows us to register the stresses more fully.

Emphasis is also achieved through alliteration. When Angelo finally abandons caution and threatens Isabella crudely, the violence of his intentions is reproduced in the hard 'd's of the alliterative phrases:

> Redeem thy brother
> By yielding up thy body to my will;
> Or else he must not only die the death,
> But thy unkindness shall his death draw out
> To ling'ring sufferance.   (II.iv.162-6)

Isabella's soliloquy, which immediately follows, includes equally striking examples:

> Yet hath he in him such a mind of honour,
> That had he twenty heads to tender down
> On twenty bloody blocks, he'd yield them up
> Before his sister should her body stoop
> To such abhorr'd pollution.   (II.iv.178-82)

Here, the alliteration conveys her confidence (misplaced, as it happens) in Claudio's moral strength.

A characteristic feature of the plays of the period is the use of sententiae. These are commonplace sayings and proverbial expressions which would have been familiar to audiences in that period. Certain dramatists, notably John Webster, used them very heavily, but Shakespeare is more sparing. Nevertheless, we find a number of examples in this play. The second line of Escalus'

> Mercy is not itself, that oft looks so;
> Pardon is still the nurse of second woe.   (II.i.280-1)

is a typical sentential. The purpose is to authenticate the view expressed; the audience accepts the authority of a sententia because it is a saying of allowed wisdom. In this example, the so/woe rhyme gives a clinching finality to the sentiments, and also serves to emphasise their good sense.

These two lines also represent an example of the Shakespearean 'doublet', in which a view is put, and then repeated in a different form. Early critics of Shakespeare, especially in the eighteenth century, sometimes criticised this kind of repetition, regarding it as unnecessary and superfluous. A further example from our play occurs when Claudio says of his sister:

> she hath prosperous art
> When she will play with reason and discourse,
> And well she can persuade.   (I.ii.174-6)

As 'prosperous' here means 'successful in the art of reasoning and discourse', the final line might be thought unnecessary. In the next scene, the Duke refers to Angelo as 'A man of stricture and firm abstinence' (I.iii.12) and the editor J. W. Lever explains 'stricture' as meaning strictness towards himself, self-repression. The two terms are therefore very close in meaning. Modern commentators very rarely complain about such overlaps of meaning; they are more often seen as enhancing the point through appropriate emphasis, especially as such overlaps are common in everyday speech.

Paradoxes (statements which appear to express contradictions) are also very popular with Shakespeare. Typical are Claudio's remarks in the prison scene:

> To sue to live, I find I seek to die,
> And seeking death, find life.   (III.i.42-3)

The literary device of paradox underlines the point that many situations contain contradictory and puzzling elements which cannot always be reconciled.

Word play and the use of puns is common. Lucio greets Pompey with the words:

> How now, noble Pompey! What, at the wheels of Caesar? Art thou led
> in triumph?   (III.ii.42-3)

where the word play consists of a reference to the historical Pompey, a famous enemy of Julius Caesar. Later in the same scene, Lucio says:

> Commend me to the prison, Pompey; you will turn good husband now, Pompey; you will keep the house.   (67-9)

where 'house' signifies both the domestic house of which he is to be a good husband (that is keeper) and the prison to which, in reality, he is being committed. There is also a reference to the brothel which he has been keeping hitherto, and which contemporaries usually referred to as a 'house'. (Early in the play we hear that 'All houses in the suburbs of Vienna must be plucked down' [I.ii.88-9]).

These puns base their appeal on comic ingenuity, but the play contains more examples of puns in wholly serious contexts. Angelo's aside, registering his desire for Isabella, is a celebrated instance:

> She speaks, and 'tis such sense
> That my sense breeds with it.   (II.ii.142-3)

The first 'sense' means 'reasonable argument'; the second 'sense' refers to his growing sexual desire.

Isabella's opening remark in the second interview with Angelo is: 'I am come to know your pleasure' (II.iv.31). Angelo replies with an aside:

> That you might know it, would much better please me,
> Than to demand what 'tis.   (II.iv.32-3)

Isabella uses 'pleasure' to mean wish or intention; Angelo deliberately misconstrues it to himself as referring to his sexual desire.

Puns are especially appropriate for *Measure for Measure*. As a major preoccupation of the work is with the concept of 'seeming', that is, false appearances, then what better way of illustrating such falsity than to show apparently innocent language turned into something more sinister and to demonstrate that the supposed certainties of semantic meaning are as ambiguous as the disguises and deceptions of human beings? Through word play, Shakespeare illustrates that hidden meanings lurk in language as well as the people who speak it. It is a world of murky perceptions.

The play also contains a number of very formal speeches, in which the language is decidedly 'literary'. The Duke's first speech to Escalus is a good example:

> Of government the properties to unfold
> Would seem in me t'affect speech and discourse,
> Since I am put to know that your own science
> Exceeds, in that, the lists of all advice
> My strength can give you.   (I.i.3-7)

The beginning of the speech with a preposition, the use of a rather ponderous vocabulary which makes the lines stately and dignified ('government', 'properties', 'speech and discourse', 'science') all suggest elaborate formality. So does the *hyperbaton* of the first line. This is a very common figure of speech in Shakespeare and describes an inversion of the ordinary order of words (we expect, 'To unfold the properties of government . . .'). The formality of language is appropriate because the event is a public occasion in which the Duke is speaking in the presence of lords and attendants. The possibility that Shakespeare is implicitly addressing James I in these lines makes their formality even more appropriate. (It is quite likely that the king would have been present at the first performance of the play at the banqueting room, Whitehall, on 26 December 1604. For further discussion of the king's relationship to the play, see 1.3 above.)

Angelo's use of the over-formal word 'fornicatress' (II.ii.23) to describe Juliet, indicates his cold and unsympathetic attitude to a pregnant woman. The Provost's 'groaning Juliet' (15) a little earlier in the scene, is much warmer and establishes a contrast between the two men.

The beginning of Isabella's campaign to secure mercy for her brother is in a highly literary and formal style also:

> There is a vice that most I do abhor,
> And most desire should meet the blow of justice;
> For which I would not plead, but that I must;
> For which I must not plead, but that I am
> At war 'twixt will and will not.   (II.ii.29-33)

This kind of repetition of phrases at the beginning and end of lines is sufficiently uncommon (as is its technical name, *symploce*) to draw special attention to Isabella's words. The repetitions underline the urgency of her pleading, constituting a stylised equivalent of the reiterated appeals of real-life begging. The stilted abstractions of the first two lines, especially the second, bring out clearly Isabella's censorious outlook.

Altogether more impressive is Isabella's celebrated speech on mercy:

> ANGELO   He's sentenced, 'tis too late.
> LUCIO (*to Isabella*)   You are too cold.
> ISABELLA   Too late? Why, no. I that do speak a word
>     May call it again. – Well, believe this:
>     No ceremony that to great ones longs,
>     Not the king's crown, nor the deputed sword,
>     The marshal's truncheon, nor the judge's robe,
>     Become them with one half so good a grace
>     As mercy does.   (II.ii.55-63)

This is very much a 'set' speech – that is, an important statement of some issue in the play delivered in a noticeably heightened style. Note especially the repeated negatives ('No ... Not ... nor ... nor ...') by which the audience's suspense increases just as the moment for being told the subject of these comparisons is delayed. The splendour of the expression from 'No ceremony ...' onwards is increased by comparison with the abrupt comments which immediately precede it from Angelo and Lucio, and Isabella's own hesitation, indicated by the clear change in her train of thought after 'again'. Angelo's perfunctory response, 'Pray you be gone' (66), has a terseness which indicates that, at least for the moment, he has no answer to her argument, and it adds to the contrast.

Claudio's use of heightened speech is interesting. There are only two undisputed examples. Here is the first:

> If I must die,
> I will encounter darkness as a bride
> And hug it in mine arms.   (III.i.82–4)

The second example also concerns a man under the threat of execution, and is said in response to a question on the whereabouts of Barnardine:

> As fast lock'd up in sleep as guiltless labour
> When it lies starkly in the traveller's bones.   (IV.ii.64–5)

Both images create a sense of immense comfort and warmth; and it is in the contrast, the pleasing incongruity between this sense and the dreadful actual predicaments of the two men which is precisely the success of the poetry.

Another 'set' speech is the Duke's disquisition on death (III.i.5–41). It is as grand as Isabella's speech on mercy, but lacks any of the latter's warmth. Shakespeare is using a number of ornate literary techniques to achieve a much colder, more analytical effect. Essentially, the style is euphuistic (so named after a work, *Euphues*, written by John Lyly in the late sixteenth century, in which this style of writing is used). The three defining characteristics are all present here. First, we find quite light alliteration: lines 7, 9, 16. Secondly, many of the sentiments are expressed antithetically; that is to say, as two counter-balancing propositions:

> For him thou labour'st by thy flight to shun,
> And yet run'st toward him still.   (12–13)

Sometimes the two propositions are, with engaging complexity, themselves divided into two:

> Thy best of rest is sleep;
> And that thou oft provok'st, yet grossly fear'st
> Thy death, which is no more.   (17–19)

Thirdly, there is a multiplicity of illustrations for what is, in effect, a simple point: that life is inevitably miserable. Earlier in his career, Shakespeare had parodied the euphuistic style (for example, in *Henry IV, Part One*) but there is no suggestion of parody here.

It is characteristic of each Shakespeare play that one type of imagery becomes especially prominent. In *Coriolanus*, political disruption is constantly compared to physical disease; *King Lear* is full of evocative metaphors based on wild animals. In *Measure for Measure*, there is a set of images based on coinage. The Duke's,

> Spirits are not finely touch'd
> But to fine issues . . .   (I.i.35-6)

is a typical example. The words 'touch'd, 'fine', and 'issues' were all used at the time in connection with the manufacture of coins. Angelo's apparent reluctance to accept the role of deputy is expressed using the same imagery:

> Let there be some more test made of my metal,
> Before so noble and so great a figure
> Be stamp'd upon it.   (I.i.48-50)

Later, Angelo refers to fornicators as those that

> do coin heaven's image
> In stamps that are forbid.   (II.iv.45-6)

Isabella describes women thus:

> For we are soft as our complexions are,
> And credulous to false prints.   (II.iv.128-9)

(The word 'print' was used, among other things, for the stamping of coins.)

The imagery of defective or suspect coinage is used in the play to emphasise Shakespeare's theme that what might appear good and whole is actually spurious and fake: the theme of 'seeming' (see 'Themes and Issues' above). It is also appropriate that this imagery is used predominantly in connection with Angelo, for the deputy's name - as well as being an ironic reminder that he is by no means an 'angel' - is also the name of a valuable coin, the angel. The falseness of Angelo is thus underlined by references to false coinage.

Shakespeare makes interesting use of the comic language of the 'low' characters. In the comic trial scene before Escalus (II.i) the Constable, Elbow, mistakes his words, often saying the opposite of what he means. Thus, malefactors become 'benefactors' (50), 'profanation' (55) is used for goodness, and the judges, Angelo and Escalus, are referred to as 'varlets' (85), Elbow clearly thinking that the term is laudatory. This is the simple comedy of Malapropism, a favourite device of Shakespeare's comedies.

Often, however, the misplacings represent ironic truths. When Elbow describes himself as 'the poor Duke's constable' (47–8) (he means, of course, the Duke's poor constable; the same mistake occurs in *Much Ado About Nothing*, with another comic law-enforcer, Dogberry, saying 'we are the poor duke's officers' [III.v.22]) he has unwittingly suggested a particular view of the Duke which, although it does not fit in with Vincentio's idea of himself, has nevertheless some validity. Similarly, the description of Angelo as a 'varlet' represents a mistake by Elbow, but it turns out prophetically to be accurate.

The exchange between Pompey and Escalus in the same scene, about prostitution, also manages to combine humour with insight:

> ESCALUS   What do you think of the trade, Pompey? Is it a lawful
>     trade?
> POMPEY   If the law would allow it, sir.
> ESCALUS   But the law will not allow it, Pompey . . . (222–5)

These remarks, and especially Pompey's, are usually cited as examples of simple-mindedness and naïvety, a comic instance of an inability to see the moral dimension to his behaviour. In this view, Pompey is an amoral creature whose only interest is to see what he can get away with; whether or not the law will allow something, irrespective of whether it is right or wrong. He is like the 'sanctimonious pirate' (I.ii.7) who discards inconvenient laws.

This is a reasonable account as far as it goes. But there is much more. Shakespeare is brilliantly illustrating the point that high-sounding moral talk usually proceeds from the mouths of those who belong to the class which makes the rules in the first place. To others, especially in the lower social strata, it is much more readily assumed that laws exist to be circumvented. It is not that the law-breakers are evil, simply that they do not recognise the authority of the system which purports to control their conduct. The magnificent contrast between the first two scenes of the play – the first full of high moral sentiment and biblical evocations, the second a jovial, bawdy scene in which we see the down-to-earth talk of brothel-frequenters – is a further example of the same contrast of attitudes.

Thus, the comic language which Shakespeare gives his characters often has a significance beyond what is immediately apparent, and often it has a serious as well as a light-hearted purpose. Even the hopelessly complicated and long-winded explanations of Pompey in this scene (88 ff.) are not merely laughable. They illustrate that truth can be obscured as well as clarified by a mass of words; something we are to witness in the altogether more heavy atmosphere of the next scene (II.ii) with its crucial interview between Angelo and Isabella.

## 5.2 STAGECRAFT

At the start of each scene, Shakespeare wants to get the audience immed-iately involved in the action, without too many tedious preliminaries. One method of ensuring this is to arrange that, at the beginning of some scenes, we are joining a conversation which has already started. The opening line is a reply to something which we are required to imagine was said before the scene started. Here are some examples:

No. Holy father, throw away that thought;   (I.iii)

And have you nuns no farther privileges?   (I.iv)

So then you hope of pardon from Lord Angelo?   (III.i)

This practice allows us to experience the scenes as fast-moving, and not as static set-pieces. We are, as it were, rushed into the action.

Of course, many speeches which do not advance the plot are included to provide the audience with information on the action. Most of I.iii is in this vein. However, Shakespeare can provide us with important details very economically. The play's opening,

DUKE   Escalus.
ESCALUS   My lord.   (I.i.1–2)

shows us in an entirely natural way (by Escalus's address, and the power of the Duke to summon him) the relationship between the two men, which would in any case be plain in the theatre by stage business: having Vincentio sitting on a throne, for instance.

*Measure for Measure* includes one of Shakespeare's favourite staging devices: the midnight-to-dawn scene. There are famous examples of this in *Hamlet*, *Othello*, *Julius Caesar* and *The Merchant of Venice*, and in this play we find it in IV.ii. We are told at line 62 that "Tis now dead midnight', and within 150 lines, 'it is almost clear dawn' (209). Obviously, the purpose of this device is to indicate that what might, in acting time, have lasted only fifteen minutes, should be taken by the audience to have lasted the whole night. But why should that sense of elongated time be so important? Certainly it creates a sense of time passing swiftly, and therefore keeps in the forefront of our minds the urgency of Claudio's predicament. Secondly, Shakespeare makes the dawn a symbol both of beauty and hope, and its description in these midnight-to-dawn scenes is often lyrical and moving, marking a change of mood from the sombre to the hopeful. In *Hamlet*, the dreadful appearance of the ghost is followed by a heightened passage which speaks of 'the morn in russet mantle clad' (I.i.166). In *Measure for Measure*, the change of mood is equally dramatic:

This is a thing that Angelo knows not; for he this very day receives letters of strange tenour, perchance of the Duke's death, perchance entering into some monastery; but, by chance, nothing of what is writ. Look, th'unfolding star calls up the shepherd. Put not yourself into amazement how these things should be; all difficulties are but easy when they are known.   (IV.ii.198–205)

To maintain audience interest, dramatists usually need to create suspense in their plays. Delaying the discovery of key information is a simple way of achieving this. For example, Angelo is made deputy in I.i, but we have to wait until I.iii to find out the reasons for this action from Vincentio.

However, Shakespeare also uses more sophisticated forms of suspense. Take, for example, the position of Angelo in V.i. We know that in this last scene he is going to be exposed. But Shakespeare is not content merely to delay this moment of discovery for a long time. He also shows Angelo, ironically, feeling safe and confident as the moment of his exposure approaches. There is a build-up in his self-assurance, which we can see in his brazen denunciation of Isabella and his insistence that she be put on trial, so that the consequent exposure is all the more of a humiliation.

Another example occurs when the Duke and the Provost are waiting at the prison for Claudio's reprieve. We are repeatedly prepared for the good news. First, the Provost hears a noise and hopes that 'it is some pardon or reprieve' (IV.ii.69). A little later, the Duke reassures the Provost that the reprieve is on its way:

> As near the dawning, Provost, as it is,
> You shall hear more ere morning.   (92–3)

Then a messenger arrives, and Vincentio's reaction is to say: 'And here comes Claudio's pardon' (99). He repeats his optimism while the message is being read: 'This is his pardon' (106). Of course, it is no reprieve at all, but a dramatic reversal; Claudio is to be executed even earlier than originally ordered. Shakespeare is here able to create an expectation which turns out to be false, and combine it with a new development of the plot.

One of Shakespeare's stock devices is the implied stage direction. We infer, from what one character says, some information about another. For example, if A says to B, 'Nay, weep not', then the actor playing B had better be weeping before A speaks. These implied stage directions are especially helpful when reading Shakespeare, as opposed to experiencing him in the theatre, because when reading the tone of a remark is not always apparent on the printed page until after it has been read. Here is a good example:

LUCIO   I hold you as a thing enskied and sainted
   By your renouncement, an immortal spirit,

>   And to be talked with in sincerity,
>   As with a saint.
> ISABELLA   You do blaspheme the good, in mocking me.   (I.iv.34–8)

Is Lucio making fun of Isabella? From what has gone before, it is very probable, but perhaps not quite certain. When we read Isabella's reply we are certain. In the theatre there is no difficulty because the actor playing Lucio will have assumed the appropriate tone of voice for the speech.

Theatrical production raises many questions which do not figure so largely when one is reading plays. Take, for example, two important 'silences' in the last scene of *Measure for Measure*. When the Duke proposes marriage to Isabella, twice, she does not reply. Readers can imagine a number of possible explanations for this or, just as likely, relegate the whole issue to the sidelines of their consciousness. But on the stage the question cannot be ignored. There must be a decision as to what, physically, Isabella is to do. Is she to smile, suggesting assent, or to give him some encouragement which is nevertheless something short of assent? Or is she to turn away crossly, or to do something, turn away gently, for example, which will indicate uncertainty and leave the problem unresolved?

Similarly, Claudio is reunited with his sister at the end, but he says not a word. Such a silence must be 'covered' by some stage business. An obvious solution is to have him rush into his sister's arms and embrace her silently.

Shakespeare was keenly aware that a play is not merely a collection of speeches but a visual experience. He therefore constantly provides opportunities for visual effects to complement the sense of the words spoken. The Courtroom scene (II.i) provides an opportunity for the sort of spectacle – for example, the use of robes and marks of office associated with judges – which emphasises the power that the judges wield. When the Provost brings in the severed head of Ragozine in IV.iii, the audience experiences a thrill of horror. In the final scene, the unveiling of Mariana, and the unmasking of the Duke, are also visually exciting moments; in addition, they reinforce the whole nature of the dénouement which is a stripping away of all disguises. Both Mariana and Isabella kneel down as they plead for mercy on Angelo's behalf, and this physical posture gives added poignancy to their words.

The locations of the scenes are extremely various: court, nunnery, prison, friar's cell, grange, and a public place near the city gates. The extensive use of the prison setting in this play not only provides a constant visual reminder of Claudio's desperate plight, but seems in tune with the gloomy tone of much of the dialogue. It is wholly appropriate that the final scene takes place out of doors, where everything that has been secret can 'come out into the open'. The outdoor setting is also appropriate for the mood of freedom in the scene (Barnardine, Claudio, Angelo and Lucio all have legal penalties remitted); the depressing claustrophobia of the prison-house is left behind.

Shakespeare exploits not only visual effects but also sound. In his plays a favourite device is knocking. The sound of Lucio knocking at the convent door (I.iv), combined with his man's voice (heard off-stage), puts the nun, Francisca, into a state of mild alarm, which audiences are likely to find amusing. Knocking is also deployed, in a more sombre context, in IV.ii, where we find Claudio and the Provost nervously waiting for the pardon from Angelo. The knocking of Angelo's messenger creates both a *frisson* and a tension. It makes both the characters, and the audiences, hold their breath. The suspense is prolonged as Shakespeare then has the messenger knock thrice more before he is admitted.

Finally we should bear in mind that, although a theatrical production is a full-bodied, three-dimensional realisation of a work which is in an incomplete form on the page, such a production is also a limiting process. In reading the play, we can keep in our minds simultaneously all the possible interpretations and ambiguities suggested by the text. On the other hand, by its very nature, a production must choose from amongst these interpretations and, as a consequence, completely exclude others.

## 5.3 CHARACTERISATION

### Isabella

At her first appearance, Isabella is seen arguing for 'a more strict restraint' (I.iv.4) upon a religious order which we know from historical record to have been particularly austere. It is thus quickly established that, like Angelo, her future antagonist, she has a strong puritanical streak. This is developed in the first interview with Angelo, when we notice the severity of her language: she calls Claudio's offence 'a vice that most I do abhor' (II.ii.29).

In temperament, she has an outward reserve which easily gives way to warmer feelings. We can see this most clearly when she is pleading for her brother's life (II.iv). Initial coyness is gradually replaced by passionate urgings, and ultimately by an insulting outburst. Linked to this excitability is what F. R. Leavis has called Isabella's 'sensuality of martyrdom'. Poets of this period, especially John Donne, frequently made a connection between religious feelings and eroticism, and we can see that connection in Isabella's words:

> were I under the terms of death,
> Th'impression of keen whips I'd wear as rubies,

> And strip myself to death as to a bed
> That longing have been sick for, ere I'd yield
> My body up to shame.   (II.iv.100–4)

The central difficulty of her character for her critics has been her attitude to Claudio. There are two chief incidents to consider here: her refusal to sacrifice her chastity, and her behaviour towards Claudio in the 'prison' scene (III.i). As to the first of these, Isabella's uncompromising 'More than our brother is our chastity' (II.iv.184) turns out to be as much a theological question as anything else. The critic J. M. Nosworthy thinks the issue is simple. If Isabella commits fornication she also commits a mortal sin, thus placing her soul in danger of eternal damnation. Compared to that fate, the death of a brother is a mere trifle. Others have expressed themselves equally strongly on the other side of the question: in refusing to save Claudio's life, Isabella is indulging in gross selfishness and exaggerated religiosity. In this view, she should have understood that God is not to be thought of as legalistic and inflexible, and would not damn her soul for sacrificing her chastity in these particular circumstances. Ernest Schanzer, who supports this line, writes: 'It never occurs to her that it would be even more monstrous a perversion of justice for God to sentence her to eternal damnation for saving a brother's life by an act that has nothing whatever in common with the deadly sin of lechery . . .'

It is clear that both Nosworthy and Schanzer are not really discussing the character of Isabella, but Renaissance theology. Their inferences about Isabella are based on theological propositions, but in both cases they are faulty. Schanzer blames Isabella for not thinking of God as a reasonable and flexible judge willing to bend his own rules and accept mitigating pleas and arguments for diminished responsibility, for all the world like a human judge. But this is very much a Protestant idea (and not widespread even then) and wholly alien to the Catholic ethos of Shakespeare's Vienna. Isabella's Catholic God is neither flexible nor 'reasonable'. It is precisely the rigidity and inflexibility of religion generally, and Catholicism in particular, in regard to moral questions, which Isabella's character illustrates. The whole story of Claudio's 'offence' and Isabella's intolerance of it is intended to show how religion makes otherwise decent people strict, undiscriminating and even ruthless.

Nosworthy is much closer to the truth but here too there is a serious omission; there is no mention of the sacrament of confession. Isabella knows full well that she could give in to Angelo and then immediately confess her sin and receive absolution and thus avoid the threat of damnation. It seems much more likely that Isabella's attitude is based not on fear of losing her soul but on her horror at the enormity of a deliberate act which would cause God the grossest offence. Nosworthy quotes Cardinal Newman here on the Catholic attitude to even venial (lesser) sins:

> The Catholic Church holds that it were better for sun and moon to drop from heaven, for the earth to fail, and for all the many millions who are upon it to die of starvation in extremest agony as far as temporal affliction goes, than that one soul, I will not say should be lost, but should [even] commit one venial sin.

The play itself, especially in II.iv, provides evidence for both the Nosworthy and Schanzer views; but the truth is that no certain or consistent answer can be found. Shakespeare was clearly not interested in sorting out the theological niceties which he nevertheless brings up in passing, through the treatment of his characters. To confuse matters still further, Isabella herself, after her confrontation with Claudio in prison (III.i) tells the Duke in the same scene: 'I had rather my brother die by the law, than my son should be unlawfully born' (188-90). The status of this new explanation (whether it is her chief consideration or merely a supplementary one) is not clear.

Having insisted on her own sexual purity, it is odd that Isabella should have no qualms about the 'bed-trick' which involves the same degree of culpability, from the religious point of view, as Claudio's offence, which Isabella finds so abhorrent. We can conclude that either she is hypocritical, or that she does not morally equate the two cases for (theological?) reasons unknown to us, or we can treat it as an inconsistency such as those described above (see 1.2).

The anger with which Isabella turns on her brother in the prison scene (III.i) is, paradoxically, far more ferocious than that directed at Angelo when the latter finally spells out his evil intention at the end of the second interview in II.iv. The mercy which Isabella begged Angelo to show is entirely absent in her own later behaviour towards her brother. Faced with a man almost paralysed with the fear of imminent death, she can only rail:

> Might but my bending down
> Reprieve thee from thy fate, it should proceed.
> I'll pray a thousand prayers for thy death;
> No word to save thee. (III.i.143-6)

The anger is hysterical, the sentiments gruesome. Shakespeare thus shows us her vices as well as her virtues and in this she is like the Duke. Happily, by the end of the play, we see her merciful side again: she pleads for Angelo's life, even though she believes that her brother has been executed.

Isabella's hectoring and sanctimonious behaviour may stem from her unworldliness. When Lucio informs her of Claudio's arrest, she cannot bring herself to believe that the story is true, even though the offence is piffling enough to the worldly. Her naïvety in the second interview with Angelo is staggering; she is simply unable to believe that he could be so wicked even when he spells out his proposal repeatedly, and so her mind refuses to take in what he is saying. (It is a well-known psychological phenomenon that information of an extremely unwelcome kind often does not register with the hearer.) In both instances, she shows complete ignorance of the nature, and ordinariness, of fleshly temptations. Hence, when she does encounter such weaknesses, she reacts with the disgust of an arid celibate theologian given to denunciations of sin. This unworldliness might also explain her silence in the face of the Duke's repeated marriage proposal in the final scene.

For one nineteenth-century critic, Mrs Jameson, Isabella has an 'angel-purity'; she is 'like a stately and graceful cedar, towering on some Alpine cliff', incapable of any 'possible lapse from virtue'. For Una Ellis-Fermor, in our century, Isabella is pitiless, inhuman, 'hard as an icicle'. We do not have to decide between these alternatives; we can say that Isabella is like real, non-fictional people in being contradictory, behaving now well, now badly, preaching mercy but not always practising it, and in general being what is ordinarily called human.

## The Duke

The nature of the Duke's character has caused a great deal of puzzlement. He represents a paradox. On the one hand, he appears as the wise prince, partly based on flattering parallels to James I (see 1.3), who sees vice and exposes it. He intervenes benignly throughout the action in order to prevent serious mishap. He comforts and counsels those in distress. He takes every opportunity to sermonise on the nature of the world and especially its evils, in terms that few in Jacobean England would quarrel with; much of what he says is based on biblical teaching or on the received wisdom of contemporary Europe. His understanding of the weaknesses of others and how they are likely to behave is almost faultless (we have to note that he fails to anticipate Angelo's order to have Claudio executed even after the assignation with Mariana). In the final scene, he skilfully engineers matters so that all the characters are forced to reveal their true moral nature: Lucio is led to exhibit his slanderous tongue, Angelo to hide his guilt in even more duplicity, Isabella to show mercy, and so on. When the final judgements are made, he tempers justice with mercy, eschewing any vindictive harshness. All this – his power, his seeming omniscience, his wisdom, his mercy, his ducal status, his piety (it is no accident that his disguise is that of a friar), but above all, the fact that he submits various characters to tests and finally to judgement – makes him seem almost god-like.

But there is, as it were, another Vincentio, one altogether more fallible. He believes himself immune to the charms of romantic love:

> Believe not that the dribbling dart of love
> Can pierce a complete bosom.   (I.iii.2–3)

But his proposal to Isabella at the end of the play shows him to have been mistaken. And there is surely something of vanity in that description of his 'complete bosom', a vanity which re-emerges in his heated reaction to Lucio's slanders ('Let him be but testimonied . . .' [III.ii.140–4]; 'No might nor greatness . . .' [179–83]).

He sets himself up as the judge of others, yet, by his own admission, he is himself at fault:

> Sith 'twas my fault to give the people scope,
> 'Twould be my tyranny to strike and gall them
> For what I bid them do . . .   (I.iii.35–7)

There is a certain irony, too, in Vincentio using lies and deception for his ends. Some of the lying, such as his pretending to Escalus that he is from Rome, 'In special business from his Holiness' (III.ii.214), or his telling Isabella that he cannot be present when the Duke returns because he is 'combined by a sacred vow' (IV.iii.144) is harmless enough. But on other occasions he causes what seems unnecessary distress. He refrains from telling Claudio in III.i that he is safe from the executioner's axe, with the result that Claudio remains in mortal fear. It could be that the Duke keeps him in ignorance to punish him for his offence with Juliet, and certainly such punishment is more lenient than execution; or he may wish to bring Claudio to a knowledge of himself by forcing him to confront the extreme of anticipating imminent death. Or it may be that Shakespeare sacrifices consistent characterisation of the Duke in order to be able to include the exciting scene in which Claudio and Isabella confront each other. We have similar problems in accounting for his delay in telling Isabella of Claudio's safety, although in this case we know a little more. First, Vincentio wants to know whether Isabella, believing her brother dead, is willing to plead for Angelo's life. Secondly, he actually offers an explanation of his behaviour:

> But I will keep her ignorant of her good,
> To make her heavenly comforts of despair
> When it is least expected.   (IV.iii.108–110)

This justification, such as it is, seems feeble and whimsical.

There are other contradictions. Throughout the play, Vincentio stresses the need for strict enforcement of the laws. It is true that, when handing over power to Angelo, he invites his deputy to 'enforce or qualify the laws' (I.i.65) where 'qualify' has the sense, 'mitigate the severity of'. But what he stresses elsewhere is the severity. He disdains fathers whose children are not beaten with the 'twigs of birch' (I.iii.24). When Lucio urges a policy of leniency towards sexual misdemeanours, Vincentio is uncompromising: 'It is too general a vice, and severity must cure it' (III.ii.96). Above all, we have to remember that the scene with Friar Thomas (I.iii) makes it clear that the chief purpose of Angelo's appointment as deputy is to do what Vincentio himself is reluctant to do: 'to strike and gall' (I.iii.36) those who break the law.

And yet, in the teeth of this, his actions in V.i are manifestly lenient. Barnardine, a worthless drunkard whose crime was capital, is released; Claudio is pardoned; Lucio is scarcely treated harshly; and the wicked Angelo gets off scot free. If we want to make sense of this in terms of the Duke's character – and, as we have seen in 1.2 above, there are cogent reasons for passing over such anomalies silently – we can say that, far from being a god-like figure, Vincentio is just like the characters whom he has been submitting to tests. He is human, fallible. At the beginning he believes in severity, but events have taught him that a softening mercy is indeed, as Isabella has pointed out to Angelo (II.ii.59-63: 'No ceremony . . .') the finest attribute of a prince.


### Angelo

Angelo's first appearance is especially impressive. He is preferred for the post of deputy above the head of Escalus, who is already established as wise and learned in the arts of government and is 'first in question' (I.i.46). The Duke describes Angelo's virtues in exaggerated, almost fulsome terms; the reference to Christ's parable of the lamp (I.i.29-35) suggests that Angelo is a truly saintly example to others. His reluctance to accept the office of deputy also reflects credit on him.

It is easy to overlook these virtues because of the play's concentration on Angelo's fall into temptation and subsequent evil conduct. He is not an intrinsically evil person who is 'found out' in the play and exposed; rather, he is someone who has built up a reputation for virtue and, until the time of the play's action, has lived an exemplary life. His weakness is similar to Isabella's: a childlike naïvety about the world of human passions, which in turn leads to a stern Puritanical outlook. One of the central points made in III.i is that human beings act not merely as a result of intellectual conviction, but also – perhaps predominantly – from emotional impulses. The rigid legalistic quibbling of Angelo is combined with an alarming new-found desire which he is ill-equipped to deal with. He makes the Duke's mistake of thinking himself immune to women's charms. Just as Vincentio's scorn for the 'dribbling dart of love' (I.iii.2) is based on a lack of self-knowledge, so Angelo's desire for Isabella is a terrible shock of self-discovery:

> Ever till now
> When men were fond, I smiled, and wonder'd how.   (II.ii.186-7)

There are monstrous villains in Shakespeare – one thinks of Iago in *Othello* and Aaron in *Titus Andronicus* – but as often there are more ordinary people who slip into wrongdoing against their better nature. Shakespeare is keen to show through such characters that once evil gets a grip, it spreads cancerously. In this respect, Angelo is similar to Macbeth. He reacts to the experience of initial temptation with horror (II.ii.162-87 'From thee . . .') but by the end of the play his original wrongdoing has led to other evils, such as threatening to use torture. In spite of the wrongs that he commits, however, there is no reason to quarrel with Isabella's view of him:

> A due sincerity govern'd his deeds
> Till he did look on me.   (V.i.444-5)

He is a man whose ascetic life-style makes him the butt of jokes. Lucio tells the disguised Duke that Angelo 'was begot between two stockfishes' (III.ii.105; stockfishes were those which had been dried out, and therefore the idea is of someone shrivelled up and lacking in sexual appeal and potency) and that 'his urine is congealed ice' (III.ii.106-7) The Duke, expressing himself with less coarseness than Lucio, says of his deputy that he

> scarce confesses
> That his blood flows; or that his appetite
> Is more to bread than stone.   (I.iii.51-3)

Because he is strict with himself, Angelo is therefore strict with others. In his impatience at the court session in II.i, and in his refusal to grant Isabella's pleas for her brother in II.ii, Angelo represents the figure of stern justice untempered by mercy. At the end of the play, he receives from Vincentio the mercy which he found himself unable to accord to others whilst he was deputy.

## Claudio

Claudio is essentially a changeable and uncertain character. At his first appearance, he tells Lucio that his punishment for having made Juliet pregnant is 'just' (I.ii.115), and he describes his behaviour as a 'thirsty evil' (122), something which 'but to speak of would offend again' (128). Almost immediately, however, he complains of Angelo's severity. He stresses that Juliet is 'fast my wife' (136) and that Angelo is showing 'tyranny' (152) towards him.

Such wavering is even more pronounced in III.i. At the beginning of the scene, he is hoping for a pardon from Angelo, but also trying to convince himself that he is ready for the worst: 'I have hope to live, and am prepar'd to die' (4). After he has heard the Duke's homily, 'Be absolute for death . . .' (5-41) he appears almost eager to die:

> To sue to live, I find I seek to die,
> And seeking death, find life. Let it come on.   (42-3)

Isabella then appears, and he reverts to a state of hope. Unable to accept his sister's statement that he must die, he asks, 'Is there no remedy?' (60). A certain resilience then seems to assert itself again:

> If I must die,
> I will encounter darkness as a bride
> And hug it in mine arms.   (82-4)

But gradually the possibility of his life being spared, even at the cost of his sister's honour, leads him to plead with Isabella to spare his life. When she rejects this plea vehemently, he changes yet again: 'I am so out of love with life that I will sue to be rid of it' (170-1).

One way of seeing Claudio is to view him as hopelessly weak, always ready with fine words of resolve but unable to hold firm for long. The abandoning of his lofty sentiments under pressure reminds us of the crumbling of Angelo's rectitude in the face of great temptation. This parallel with Angelo is strengthened by the fact that Claudio actually echoes the deputy's earlier arguments. When he claims:

> What sin you do to save a brother's life,
> Nature dispenses with the deed so far
> That it becomes a virtue.   (133-5)

we cannot help thinking of Angelo's:

> Might there not be a charity in sin
> To save this brother's life?   (II.iv.63-4)

There is a second, kinder way of viewing Claudio, which involves recognising just how extreme is the pressure under which he has been placed. Under threat of death, and with the possibility of evading the sentence, it may be that not only the very weak would behave as he does.

It is curious that, although his dramatic reappearance in the final scene is one of the chief moments of the dénouement, he never speaks. It has been suggested that this is because Shakespeare found Claudio an unsympathetic character and kept him silent to avoid glamorising his rescue. It is just as likely to be an oversight on the part of the dramatist. At any rate, the silence needs to be 'covered' by some stage business.

## Lucio

When we first see Lucio, he is amongst his cronies, engaging in raillery and bawdy joking. He is quite at ease in the company of the brothel-keepers and their customers; he is no doubt a customer himself.

From the very start, therefore, he is associated with sexual licence, and provides a stark contrast to the more serious characters who condemn sexual irregularities, sometimes (in the case of Angelo and Isabella) with almost fanatical zeal. Claudio's fornication with Juliet is, for Isabella, 'a vice that most I do abhor' (II.ii.29) and for Angelo, it is one of the 'filthy vices' (II.iv.42). For the Duke, lechery is 'too general a vice, and severity must cure it' (III.ii.96). As a foil to all these, Lucio accepts his friend Claudio's deed as wholly natural. When Isabella asks him the reason for her brother's imprisonment, he answers:

> For that which, if myself might be his judge,
> He should receive his punishment in thanks:
> He hath got his friend with child.   (I.iv.27-9)

Later, he is more expansive in conversation with the disguised Duke:

> Why, what a ruthless thing is this in him, for the rebellion of a codpiece to take away the life of a man!   (III.ii.110-12)

What for Angelo, Isabella and Vincentio is 'vice', is for Lucio 'sport' (III.ii.116) It is therefore a marvellous irony that the rakish Lucio should combine forces with the puritanical Isabella in order to plead for mercy for Claudio.

That Lucio should go to considerable lengths to help to save Claudio's life illustrates that he has loyalty to a friend. However, that loyalty does not stretch to another friend, Pompey. When the latter is under arrest, Lucio not only refuses to stand bail, but actually humiliates the friend who is now in distress:

> How now, noble Pompey! What, at the wheels of Caesar?
> Art thou led in triumph?   (III.ii.42-3)

Rather less repellent for the audience, because it is also very funny, is Lucio's slandering of the Duke, without realising that he is doing so in the presence of Vincentio himself. We are so used to political slanders in our own age that it is difficult to understand how seriously slander was treated in Shakespeare's time. Most particularly, the slandering of the monarch could, in certain cases, lead to capital punishment. Lucio's motives for his slanders are not completely clear, but it appears that they are a combination of two features. First, he wishes to appear to be a person important enough to know even the Duke intimately. It is a question of personal vanity and he returns to it on several occasions: 'I was an inward of his'

(III.ii.127); 'Sir, I know him and love him' (145); 'my name is Lucio, well known to the Duke' (155) and so on. Secondly, there is a quality of mockery in the slanders which, however, is not quite strong enough to be called malice, and of which we saw signs at his first appearance in the play.

Just as Shakespeare uses the comic trial scene with Pompey and Froth (II.i) to point up the themes in the more serious parts of the play, so the role of Lucio has a wider significance. His bad treatment of Mistress Kate Keep-down, leading to his being forced by the Duke in the final scene to marry her, provides of course a direct parallel with Angelo's experience with Mariana. Equally important, he is unlike the play's three major characters (Angelo, Isabella and Vincentio) in that he does not judge others. He already knows the lesson that the others have to learn through bitter experience.

His healthy brashness and impudence – he constantly interrupts the Duke in the final scene – provides a refreshing contrast to the hidebound legalistic preoccupations of the morally righteous characters. It is no accident that it is Lucio who pulls off Lodowick's hood and 'exposes' the Duke's true identity. This incident is a powerful symbol of intrigue and pretence being stripped away. But, in so far as Lucio is by no means above reproach, his action in uncovering the Duke proves to be his own undoing.

## General Points

It is often noted that the major characters in *Measure for Measure* do not always engage our attention in the same way as in other Shakespeare plays. They seem at times to be a little flat, less psychologically rounded out. This might be because, especially in the first half, the play is very much one of ideas, and Shakespeare seems to be concentrating more on abstract notions such as justice, deception and good government, than on portraying entirely believable people.

The minor characters reflect both the play's themes and the major characters. Thus, Escalus's comments – for example, 'Some rise by sin, and some by virtue fall' (II.i.38) – often have an authoritative, proverbial ring, which contrasts with the unattractive severity of Angelo. The comic malapropisms of Elbow (his name suggests a physical clumsiness mirroring his verbal incompetence) are an obvious illustration of the play's preoccupation with falseness, with things not meaning what they seem to mean. Abhorson's passing judgement on Pompey, although he himself is by no means perfect, parallels Angelo's passing judgement on Claudio. The dissoluteness of Barnardine and Froth seem an (at times exaggerated) echo of Lucio's self-centred libertinism. Mariana's unshakeable firmness in her love for Angelo is contrasted with Angelo's own failure to be virtuous. Shakespeare establishes both the Provost and Escalus as solid, responsible and wise; they act as a sort of bench-mark against which we can see all the clearer how far Angelo has departed from the just norm, in his severity towards Claudio.

# 6 SPECIMEN PASSAGE AND COMMENTARY

ANGELO    Believe me, on mine honour,                    146
    My words express my purpose.
ISABELLA    Ha? Little honour, to be much believ'd,
    And most pernicious purpose! Seeming, seeming!
    I will proclaim thee, Angelo, look for't.
    Sign me a present pardon for my brother,
    Or with an outstretch'd throat I'll tell the world aloud
    What man thou art.
ANGELO    Who will believe thee, Isabel?
    My unsoil'd name, th'austereness of my life,
    My vouch against you, and my place i'th'state
    Will so your accusation overweigh,                    156
    That you shall stifle in your own report,
    And smell of calumny. I have begun,
    And now I give my sensual race the rein:
    Fit thy consent to my sharp appetite;
    Lay by all nicety and prolixious blushes
    That banish what they sue for. Redeem thy brother
    By yielding up thy body to my will;
    Or else he must not only die the death,
    But thy unkindness shall his death draw out
    To ling'ring sufferance. Answer me tomorrow,          166
    Or, by the affection that now guides me most,
    I'll prove a tyrant to him. As for you,
    Say what you can: my false o'erweighs your true.
ISABELLA    To whom should I complain? Did I tell this,
    Who would believe me? O perilous mouths,
    That bear in them one and the self-same tongue
    Either of condemnation or approof,
    Bidding the law make curtsey to their will,

Hooking both right and wrong to th'appetite,
To follow as it draws! I'll to my brother.                    176
Though he hath fall'n by prompture of the blood,
Yet hath he in him such a mind of honour,
That had he twenty heads to tender down
On twenty bloody blocks, he'd yield them up
Before his sister should her body stoop
To such abhorr'd pollution.
Then, Isabel live chaste, and brother, die:
More than our brother is our chastity.
I'll tell him yet of Angelo's request,
And fit his mind to death, for his soul's rest.               186
                              (II.iv.146-86)

This passage, at the very end of Act II, shows both Angelo and Isabella at a pitch of emotional intensity, which contrasts with the relative restraint of much of what has gone before in the scene.

There is a double irony in Angelo's opening comment. First, in a desperate bid to ensure that Isabella understands that he is in earnest in his threat, he uses the phrase 'on mine honour' – and what a hollow ring that has in the mouth of a man capable of such baseness! Secondly, his assurance that what he says 'expresses his purpose' makes a dramatic contrast with the sustained evasions of the dialogue up to this point. Isabella's answer, with its explicit reference to 'seeming', draws attention to one of the most significant themes of the play: people pretending to be what they are not. It also gives the lie to the notion, presented by some critics, that Isabella is a meek, submissive figure. The last three lines of this speech (151-3) constitute a vigorous counter-threat. They prefigure the Isabella who, when deceived by Angelo over Claudio's release, is able to cry in rage, 'O, I will to him and pluck out his eyes!' (IV.iii.119).

One can divide Shakespearean speeches into many categories. For present purposes, I should like to draw attention to the difference between what I shall call 'static' and 'dynamic' types. Static speeches tend to have one predominant mood and the speaker gives a sense of having thought through all the points about to be made before commencing. (See, for example, I.i.26-47, 'Angelo:/There is a kind of character . . .'; I.iii.19-31, 'We have strict statues . . .'; III.i.5-41, 'Be absolute for death . . .'.) To put it another way, there is no emotional development in the speakers during the course of such speeches. Both of the speeches we now have under consideration, by contrast, constitute records of thinking as it is taking place. Instead of being static they are dynamic. Thus, in Angelo's speech, the first six lines are concerned with countering Isabella's threat to expose him. At line 158 ('I have begun . . .') he moves on to another area of concern and adopts an approach which, it is clear, has just come into his mind – something underlined by the use of 'now' (159). Similarly, in Isabella's speech, her decision, 'I'll to my brother', clearly arises out of the predicament she describes and is reacting to in the preceding lines.

Angelo's speech is a reaction to Isabella's threat, and his tersely triumphant 'Who will believe thee, Isabel?' is in marked contrast to the ingratiating and insinuating tones which he has been using up to this moment. The strength of his case, and his conviction that he is safe from exposure, are conveyed by the confidence involved in his use of 'my' four times, and by the crescendo of arguments he marshalls against her (154–8). One notes in particular the first two of these lines and how each is so neatly divided into two, creating a rhythm which stresses the weight of the points contained in them:

> My unsoil'd name, th'austereness of my life,
> My vouch against you, and my place i'th'state

The violence of Angelo's purpose is appropriately conveyed in strong physical images: 'stifle', 'smell of calumny', 'sensual race the rein', and especially, 'my sharp appetite' (much sexual slang, then and now, is based on metaphors of eating).

Angelo's ruthlessness, and his intimidating threats, are skilfully registered by the use of verbs in the imperative mood – that is, verbs giving commands: 'Fit thy consent', 'Lay by all nicety', 'Redeem thy brother', 'Answer me tomorrow', 'Say what you can'.

The lines in which he urges Isabella to abandon any idea of resistance are especially interesting:

> Lay by all nicety and prolixious blushes
> That banish what they sue for . . .

First of all, this reminds us of what he says in soliloquy at the end of the first meeting with Isabella; namely, that it is precisely her 'nicety', her maiden modesty, which stirs his desire ('Dost thou desire her foully for those things/That make her good?' [II.ii.174–5]) Secondly, the lines are usually taken to mean that blushes are forms of modesty which, instead of preventing the admirer from making an advance, actually have the opposite effect and encourage such an advance. However, there is surely also a suggestion behind Angelo's comment that the nicety and blushes are fake, put on by Isabella in order to tantalise him whilst at the same time remaining within the safe confines of demure and proper conduct. Angelo is of course mistaken in thinking this; but in his state of high agitation he reveals a common symptom of the sexually frustrated: their belief that the unattainable object of their desire is deliberately engaged in sexual teasing, which they then strongly resent.

The whole speech has a sort of momentum; he is working himself up into a state of intense feeling. It is because of the resulting emotional instability that he is led to threaten not only to take Claudio's life, but to torture him. The violence of the threats comes through in the alliterative effects: 'die the death', 'death draw out'. We feel here that Angelo's viciousness is uncharacteristic, a distortion of his ordinary self. We believe Isabella is correct later when she says of him that 'A due sincerity govern'd his deeds/Till he did look on me' (V.i.444-5).

Such a sentiment also fits with the Duke's praise of him at the beginning of the play, which is surely based on sound knowledge and observation. Angelo is a virtuous man who has fallen into evil, not someone already wicked, like Iago in *Othello*, who earns a reputation for honesty merely through clever deception.

Angelo describes Isabella's attitude as 'unkindness'. It is not certain whether he intends to refer to her unkindness towards himself, or towards her own brother in not saving his life, or perhaps both. The word 'unkind' was much stronger in meaning in Shakespeare's day, and suggested the gross, especially unnatural behaviour between relatives. The irony of the word is therefore that, although Isabella can be seen as showing unkindness by resisting Angelo, she would also be showing it by giving in to him and committing an unnatural act.

Angelo insists that Isabella 'Answer me tomorrow'. Shakespeare's great eagerness to emphasise the swift onrush of events in this play can be seen in this 'tomorrow'. In connection with Claudio's execution, there are fourteen references to 'tomorrow' and three further references to the imminence of his death. In the sources on which Shakespeare drew for his play, the corrupt judge allows several days to his victim; Shakespeare has deliberately altered this to one day.

Angelo concludes by claiming that 'my false o'erweighs your true.' J. W. Lever suggests that the reference is to false coins, which are physically lighter than their genuine counterparts. Therefore the phrase would be a paradox; we expect that the true, being heavier, will outweigh the false. Shakespeare and his contemporaries had a particular fondness for paradox as a literary device, and there are many other examples in this play (see 5.1 above, 'Language'). The use of paradox underlines, of course, the point that it is often difficult to see clearly where the truth lies in any given situation.

Once alone, Isabella's distress is made more poignant by the use of the two despairing rhetorical questions, addressed to herself, with which her speech opens. Then, as so very often happens in Shakespeare, we pass from the specific example to the general rule. She comments on those who would, like Angelo, seize what they desire, whether it is right or wrong. These lines ('O perilous mouths . . . To follow as it draws') are colder and more analytical in mood than what she goes on to say. It is almost as if, for a moment, she is speaking on the subject of human weaknesses with the Duke's superior detachment.

In the lines expressing confidence in her brother – ironic, of course, because misplaced – her strength of feeling is well rendered in the allitera- tive sounds of 179 and 180. Indeed, the whole section from 179 to 184 has an assertive violence of emotion, especially the words 'abhorr'd pollu- tion', which reminds us of how, earlier in the scene, she had expressed a similar intensity:

> . . . were I under the terms of death,
> Th'impression of keen whips I'd wear as rubies,
> And strip myself to death as to a bed
> That longing have been sick for, ere I'd yield
> My body up to shame.   (100-4)

The concluding four lines of Isabella's speech constitute a masterpiece of decrescendo. We can feel her cooling down in their calm serenity; this is especially noticeable in the last line which is, one notes in passing, yet another of the many references in the play to the rest/death comparison.

But if there is calmness, there is also firm determination; one might even say, rigidity. You can hear it in

> Then, Isabel live chaste, and brother, die

with its three pauses and coldly systematic rhythm. This is followed by the thrilling resolution of

> More than our brother is our chastity

which, amongst other things, enlists the audience's sympathy anew for Claudio, and presents us with yet another line in which the predominant feature of the speaker's character is strong, simple determination.

# 7 CRITICAL RECEPTION

It is only in the present century that *Measure for Measure* has been favoured. The history of critical reaction to *Measure for Measure* is one of sustained distaste and, not infrequently, hostility. For John Dryden, the play was 'meanly written' and another seventeenth-century commentator complained that the language was sometimes 'rough and obsolete' and that Shakespeare was too rambling and repetitive.

But the chief early criticisms stemmed from a dislike of the basic structure and meaning of the play, as these were perceived. Dryden thought the plot 'grounded upon impossibilities' and the comic parts unsuccessful. His conclusion was 'that the comedy neither caused your mirth, nor the serious part your concernment'.

Charles Gildon, writing in 1710, praised the work's moral: 'a just satire against our present reformers who would alter their course of nature and bring us to a perfection mankind never knew ... The main story ... is truly tragical, for it is adapted to move terror and compassion.'

Perhaps the angriest reaction of the century came from Charlotte Lennox in 1753: 'Shakespeare ... is greatly below the novelist, since the incidents he has added [to the source material] are neither necessary nor probable.' She was especially angry that Angelo was not properly punished. Shakespeare 'shows vice not only pardoned but left in tranquility. The cruel, the vicious and the hypocritical Angelo marries a fair and virtuous woman who tenderly loved him.' What was a tragic story in the sources, Shakespeare 'was resolved to torture into a comedy'. That the tragi-comic combination was not successful was clear from 'the low contrivance, absurd intrigue and improbable incidents he was obliged to introduce in order to bring about three or four weddings instead of one good beheading, which was the consequence naturally expected'. She adds for good measure, 'I cannot see the use of all that juggling and ambiguity at the winding up of the catastrophe.'

Dr Johnson shared Charlotte Lennox's annoyance at Angelo's escape from punishment. The moral and didactic purposes of literature are to the fore as he makes the routine points: 'Angelo's crimes were such, as must sufficiently justify punishment, whether its end be to secure the innocent from wrong, or to deter guilt by example: and I believe every reader feels some indignation when he finds him spared.'

Johnson is also unhappy about Isabella's reasons for pleading for mercy on Angelo's behalf. He cannot bring himself to believe that Isabella could be moved solely by the spirit of forgiveness and proposes his own alternative, which is that Shakespeare was trying to demonstrate 'that women think ill of nothing that raises the credit of their beauty, and are ready, however virtuous, to pardon any act which they think incited by their own charms'. On the play as a whole, his reaction was mixed: 'the light or comic part is very natural and pleasing, but the grave scenes, if a few passages be expected, have more labour than elegance. The plot is rather intricate than artful.'

Nineteenth-century criticism is more pro-Isabella than modern criticism. Mrs Jameson, in *Shakespeare's Heroines* (1886) says that 'Isabel is like a stately and graceful cedar, towering on some Alpine cliff, unbowed and unscathed amid the storm . . . her spirit seems to stand upon an eminence, and look down upon the world as if already enskied and sainted . . ..' The celebrated German critic A. W. Schlegel believed that 'the heavenly purity of her mind is not even stained with one unholy thought: in the humble robes of the novice she is a very angel of light.' Edward Dowden in 1875 finds in her a 'virginal strength and severity and beauty'. Writers who were not as enthusiastic as this nevertheless come down very lightly on Isabella. William Hazlitt merely says that he is not 'greatly enamoured of Isabella's rigid chastity, though she could not act otherwise than she did'. The Romantic poet  S. T. Coleridge contents himself by describing her as 'unaimiable'.

On the play as a whole, however, Coleridge is severe: the tragic parts were 'horrible', and the comic parts 'disgusting'. Claudio is 'detestable'. The merciful ending he especially resents: 'It is a hateful work . . . Our feelings of justice are grossly wounded in Angelo's escape . . ..' The poet Swinburne was also angry at Angelo's escape from punishment.

In the twentieth century, we can identify two main schools of thought. We have in the first place those critics who look at the play as cynical. E. K. Chambers talked of 'a puzzled and disturbed spirit, full of questioning, sceptical of its own ideals', and Dover Wilson wrote of 'weariness' and 'discord'. Una Ellis-Fermor developed the view that it was the Jacobean age itself which was full of the 'dread of death and horror of life', 'all-comprehending doubt', 'a dead disgust', and so on.

A second group of critics, who only start to appear in the 1930s, stress that the play is a statement of the Christian ethic. The most influential statement of this position was in G. Wilson Knight's essay on the play in *The Wheel of Fire* (1930), although Roy Battenhouse and Nevill Coghill elaborated the argument. The play was seen as a parable such as those found in the New Testament: Vincentio, the merciful Duke, represents God; Lucio, because he mocks the good and does evil, represents the devil. Great emphasis was placed on the lines in the play which refer to biblical passages.

Interpretations emphasising the play's interest in commercialism are also popular, though with fewer adherents. Typical of such contemporary critics is Richard Wilson. He cites the imagery (especially of coinage), Angelo's name (an Angel was an English gold coin) and the concern shared by Claudio and Angelo over the payment of dowries, to show that in the play 'sexual and emotional relations are reduced to terms of "ready money"'.

The theme of religious fanaticism (as illustrated in different degrees by Angelo and Isabella) has, not surprisingly in view of recent British political and social history, played a far greater part than in earlier criticism.

Most conspicuously, the play – along with other 'problem' comedies, especially *Troilus and Cressida* – is much more popular than it has ever been, and this may well be owing to the modernist and post-modernist appetite for ambiguity, mixed genre works, and the inherently contradictory.

# REVISION QUESTIONS

1. 'The respective merits of justice and mercy are explored in the play, but no overall view emerges at the end.' Discuss.

2. Ruthless puritan or saintly heroine? What is your view of Isabella?

3. Examine the dramatic function of the play's comic scenes.

4. 'The Duke is not a godlike figure, or a benign presence, but an unsympathetic and deceiving bungler.' Do you agree?

5. Discuss the play's attitude to different forms of sexual conduct.

6. Lucio is hardly a virtuous figure, and yet he is consistently found likeable by readers and, more especially, audiences. How do you account for this?

7. Discuss the influence of the New Testament on the language and the plot of *Measure for Measure*.

8. 'He was not an evil man; merely a weak one who fell into temptation.' Examine this view of Angelo.

9. Examine the role of Escalus in the play.

10. What makes *Measure for Measure* a 'problem' play?

11. Do you feel that there is a strong degree of cynicism in this work?

12. Until quite recently in this century, *Measure for Measure* has not been a popular play for readers or audiences. What do you think are the reasons?

13. F. R. Leavis claimed that the Duke's views and attitudes are, in all respects, meant to be ours. Discuss this view.

# APPENDIX :

# SHAKESPEARE'S THEATRE

# BY HAROLD BROOKS

We should speak, as Muriel Bradbrook reminds us, not of the Elizabethan stage but of Elizabethan stages. Plays of Shakespeare were acted on tour, in the halls of mansions, one at least in Gray's Inn, frequently at Court, and after 1609 at the Blackfriars, a small, roofed theatre for those who could afford the price. But even after his Company acquired the Blackfriars, we know of no play of his not acted (unless, rather improbably, *Troilus* is an exception) for the general public at the Globe, or before 1599 at its predecessor, The Theatre, which, since the Globe was constructed from the same timbers, must have resembled it. Describing the Globe, we can claim therefore to be describing, in an acceptable sense, Shakespeare's theatre, the physical structure his plays were designed to fit. Even in the few probably written for a first performance elsewhere, adaptability to that structure would be in his mind.

For the facilities of the Globe we have evidence from the drawing of the Swan theatre (based on a sketch made by a visitor to London about 1596) which depicts the interior of another public theatre; the builder's contract for the Fortune theatre, which in certain respects (fortunately including the dimensions and position of the stage) was to copy the Globe; indications in the dramatic texts; comments, like Ben Jonson's on the throne let down from above by machinery; and eye-witness testimony to the number of spectators (in round figures, 3000) accommodated in the auditorium.

In communicating with the audience, the actor was most favourably placed. Soliloquising at the centre of the front of the great platform, he was at the mid-point of the theatre, with no one among the spectators more than sixty feet away from him. That platform-stage (Figs I and II) was the most important feature for performance at the Globe. It had the audience – standing in the yard (10) and seated in the galleries (9) – on three sides of it. It was 43 feet wide, and 27½ feet from front to back. Raised (?5½ feet) above the level of the yard, it had a trap-door (II.8)

# SHAKESPEARE'S THEATRE
The stage and its adjuncts; the tiring-house; and the auditorium.

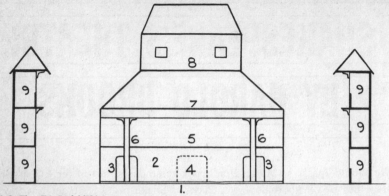

FIG I  ELEVATION
1. Platform stage (approximately five feet above the ground)  2. Tiring-house
3. Tiring-house doors to stage  4. Conjectured third door  5. Tiring-house
gallery (balustrade and partitioning not shown)  6. Pillars supporting the
heavens  7. The heavens  8. The hut  9. The spectators' galleries

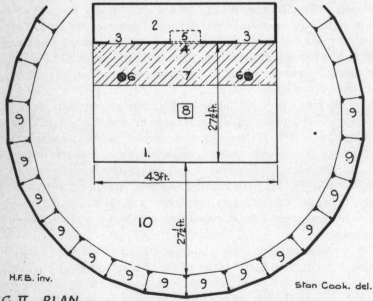

H.F.B. inv.                                        Stan Cook. del.

FIG II  PLAN
1. Platform stage  2. Tiring-house  3. Tiring-house doors to stage
4. Conjectural third door  5. Conjectural discovery space (alternatively behind 3)
6. Pillars supporting the heavens  7. The heavens  8. Trap door  9. Spectators'
gallery  10. The yard

The Globe

**An artist's imaginative recreation of a typical Elizabethan theatre**

giving access to the space below it. The actors, with their equipment, occupied the 'tiring house' (attiring-house: 2) immediately at the back of the stage. The stage-direction 'within' means inside the tiring-house. Along its frontage, probably from the top of the second storey, juts out the canopy or 'Heavens', carried on two large pillars rising through the platform (6, 7) and sheltering the rear part of the stage, the rest of which, like the yard, was open to the sky. If the 'hut' (I.8), housing the machinery for descents, stood, as in the Swan drawing, above the 'Heavens', that covering must have had a trap-door, so that the descents could be made through it.

Descents are one illustration of the vertical dimension the dramatist could use to supplement the playing-area of the great platform. The other opportunities are provided by the tiring-house frontage or facade. About this facade the evidence is not as complete or clear as we should like, so that Fig. I is in part conjectural. Two doors giving entry to the platform there certainly were (3). A third (4) is probable but not certain. When curtained, a door, most probably this one, would furnish what must be termed a discovery-space (II.5), not an inner stage (on which action in any depth would have been out of sight for a significant part of the audience). Usually no more than two actors were revealed (exceptionally, three), who often then moved out on to the platform. An example of this is Ferdinand and Miranda in *The Tempest* 'discovered' at chess, then seen on the platform speaking with their fathers. Similarly the gallery (I.5) was not an upper stage. Its use was not limited to the actors: sometimes it functioned as 'lords' rooms' for favoured spectators, sometimes, perhaps, as a musician's gallery. Frequently the whole gallery would not be needed for what took place aloft: a window-stage (as in the first balcony scene in *Romeo*, even perhaps in the second) would suffice. Most probably this would be a part (at one end) of the gallery itself; or just possibly, if the gallery did not (as it does in the Swan drawing) extend the whole width of the tiring-house, a window over the left or right-hand door. As the texts show, whatever was presented aloft, or in the discovery-space, was directly related to the action on the platform, so that at no time was there left, between the audience and the action of the drama, a great bare space of platform-stage. In relating Shakespeare's drama to the physical conditions of the theatre, the primacy of that platform is never to be forgotten.

*Note*: The present brief account owes most to C. Walter Hodges, *The Globe Restored*; Richard Hosley in *A New Companion to Shakespeare Studies*, and in *The Revels History of English Drama*; and to articles by Hosley and Richard Southern in *Shakespeare Survey*, 12, 1959, where full discussion can be found.

HAROLD BROOKS

# FURTHER READING

**Editions of the Play**
(with useful introductions and notes)
The New Arden edition, ed. J. W. Lever (Methuen, 1965)
The New Penguin edition, ed. J. M. Nosworthy (1969)

**Books on the Play**
Lascelles, Mary, *Shakespeare's 'Measure for Measure'* (London: Athlone Press, 1953)
Stevenson, David L., *The Achievement of Shakespeare's 'Measure for Measure'* (Cornell: Cornell University Press, 1968)

**Books on Shakespeare which contain substantial comment on *Measure for Measure***
Knight, G. Wilson, *The Wheel of Fire* (London: Oxford University Press, 1930)
Leavis, F. R., *The Common Pursuit* (London: Chatto & Windus, 1952)
Lawrence, W. W., *Shakespeare's Problem Comedies* (London: Macmillan, 1931)
Stoll, E. E., *From Shakespeare to Joyce* (New York: Doubleday, 1944)
Schanzer, Ernest, *The Problem Plays of Shakespeare* (Routledge & Kegan Paul, 1963)
Ure, Peter, *Shakespeare's Problem Plays* (London: Longman, 1961)

**Collections of critical essays containing criticism of *Measure for Measure***
Stead, C. K. (ed.) *Shakespeare: 'Measure for Measure'*, Casebook Series (London: Macmillan, 1971)
Palmer, D. J., *Shakespeare's Later Comedies* (Harmondsworth: Penguin, 1971)

## Mastering English Literature
Richard Gill

*Mastering English Literature* will help readers both to enjoy English Literature and to be successful in 'O' levels, 'A' levels and other public exams. It is an introduction to the study of poetry, novels and drama which helps the reader in four ways - by providing ways of approaching literature, by giving examples and practice exercises, by offering hints on how to write about literature, and by the author's own evident enthusiasm for the subject. With extracts from more than 200 texts, this is an enjoyable account of how to get the maximum satisfaction out of reading, whether it be for formal examinations or simply for pleasure.

## Work Out English Literature ('A' level)
S.H. Burton

This book familiarises 'A' level English Literature candidates with every kind of test which they are likely to encounter. Suggested answers are worked out step by step and accompanied by full author's commentary. The book helps students to clarify their aims and establish techniques and standards so that they can make appropriate responses to similar questions when the examination pressures are on. It opens up fresh ways of looking at the full range of set texts, authors and critical judgements and motivates students to know more of these matters.

8560868053856 08